简化

太极拳

理论与实践

主　编 • 吴　昊
副主编 • 张旭光

北京大学出版社
PEKING UNIVERSITY PRESS

图书在版编目(CIP)数据

简化太极拳理论与实践/吴昊主编. —北京：北京大学出版社，2017.1
ISBN 978-7-301-26833-9

Ⅰ.①简… Ⅱ.①吴… Ⅲ.①太极拳—教材 Ⅳ.①G852.11

中国版本图书馆 CIP 数据核字（2016）第 025108 号

书　　名	简化太极拳理论与实践 JIANHUA TAIJIQUAN LILUN YU SHIJIAN
著作责任者	吴　昊　主编
责任编辑	桂　春
标准书号	ISBN 978-7-301-26833-9
出版发行	北京大学出版社
地　　址	北京市海淀区成府路 205 号　100871
网　　址	http://www.pup.cn　新浪微博：@北京大学出版社
电子信箱	zyjy@pup.cn
电　　话	邮购部 62752015　发行部 62750672　编辑部 62756923
印 刷 者	北京中科印刷有限公司
经 销 者	新华书店
	787 毫米×1092 毫米　16 开本　13 印张　316 千字 2017 年 1 月第 1 版　2023 年 8 月第 3 次印刷
定　　价	31.00 元

未经许可，不得以任何方式复制或抄袭本书之部分或全部内容。
版权所有，侵权必究
举报电话：010-62752024　电子信箱：fd@pup.pku.edu.cn
图书如有印装质量问题，请与出版部联系，电话：010-62756370

前　言

随着人类文化与文明相互间学习、交流、融合的加深,中国文化越来越得到世界各国人民的欢迎,越来越多的外国朋友爱上了中国文化,全球兴起了"中国热",刮起了"中国风"。

太极拳是中国传统文化的结晶和代表,自创始至今已有近百年的历史。据不完全统计,包括中国在内,全球150多个国家和地区练习太极拳者已近3亿人。太极拳作为中国文化的产物,强调内涵文化的传承、精神修为和养生之道,其蕴含的宇宙观、价值观、人生观等对人的成长与发展具有积极意义。习练太极拳,除了要掌握太极拳的动作与套路,更重要的是通过练拳以实现文化传承、健体养心、完全人格。

作为工作在大学体育教育战线的教师和教学管理人员,编者一直致力于编写一本理论与实践相结合,较系统适用于中外学习者使用的太极拳教材。本书有以下特点。

一、突出文化性,强调实效与适用。增加了拳理和拳法内容,以提高习练者的人文底蕴,掌握太极拳学练规律和自修方法。

二、尽量展示太极拳的多元特点,使习练者在短期内尽可能完整地了解、掌握太极拳的基本技能、技法。

三、加强了太极拳基本功、基础训练以及教学方法的内容,在有限的课时内,最大限度地保证太极拳教学内容的完整性和实效性。

四、第四章、第五章附有套路练习的对照英文(英文部分 fig×-×同中文部分图×-×),以更好满足国外学习者的需求。

本书第一章第二节由刘林青编写;第四章、第七章由对外经济贸易大学张旭光编写。第四、五章的英文翻译由对外经济贸易大学英语学院阎彬老师完成,图片摄影由王焕宇、龚建新完成。其余内容由北京大学体育部吴昊编写。本书出版之际,感谢北京大学教务部的大力支持!此外,对教材编写过程中,龚欣瑜、叶月所做的文字整理、校对工作也一并表示感谢!

鉴于编者水平所限,加之时间紧促,书中如有错漏之处,恳请批评斧正。

编者

2016年11月23日

目 录

- 第一章 太极拳概论 ·· (1)
  - 第一节 太极拳起源与流派形成 ·· (1)
  - 第二节 太极拳特点与功用 ·· (4)
- 第二章 太极拳知识与要点 ·· (8)
  - 第一节 太极拳之意、气、形、神 ·· (8)
  - 第二节 练习太极拳对身体部位的要求 ······································ (11)
  - 第三节 太极拳基本技法要领 ·· (13)
- 第三章 太极拳基础动作及要领 ·· (19)
  - 第一节 基础动作 ·· (19)
  - 第二节 太极拳运臂练习 ·· (31)
  - 第三节 太极拳行步练习 ·· (40)
  - 第四节 太极拳推手练习 ·· (44)
- 第四章 九式太极操 ·· (55)
  - 第一节 创编原则及要领 ·· (55)
  - 第二节 练习目标及重点 ·· (58)
  - 第三节 动作方法及要领 ·· (59)
- 第五章 简化太极拳套路 ·· (119)
- 第六章 简化太极拳健身指导 ·· (168)
  - 第一节 锻炼方法和技术指导 ·· (168)
  - 第二节 太极拳练习时的注意事项及常见损伤与预防 ············ (170)
  - 第三节 太极拳训练时的易犯错误及纠正方法 ························ (172)
  - 第四节 技术发展不同阶段的要求 ·· (174)
- 第七章 太极拳的教学特点与学练方法 ·· (176)
  - 第一节 太极拳教学特点 ·· (176)
  - 第二节 太极拳学练方法 ·· (179)
- 附录一 古传《太极拳论》及经典歌诀 ·· (185)
- 附录二 武术(太极拳)段位入段指南 ·· (189)
- 附录三 太极拳竞赛规则 ·· (191)
- 参考文献 ·· (199)

第一章 太极拳概论

本章介绍了太极拳的起源与五大流派（陈式、杨式、吴式、武式和孙式）的形成及各自特点。太极拳以其丰富的技术风格、独特的技击特点、显著的健身价值、鲜明的文化特性和广泛的传播方式，越来越受国人乃至全世界人民的瞩目和喜爱，人们借由太极拳修身养性、以武明德的同时，也极大地促进了太极文化的传承与发展。

第一节 太极拳起源与流派形成

太极拳运动在中国历史悠久，流派众多，其中流传较广、特点较为显著的有陈式、杨式、吴式、武式和孙式。二十四式太极拳是第一套由国家统一规定、按国际标准创编的太极拳套路，它是原中国国家体委武术处（现中国国家体育总局武术研究院）于1955年组织部分太极拳专家，在继承传统杨式太极拳的基础上，删繁就简，按照由易到难、由简入繁、循序渐进的原则，经过反复论证而创编的。

二十四式太极拳突出太极拳的健身性和大众普及性，它的推出使太极拳走进大众健身领域，是太极拳运动史上一个划时代的革新。

目前，太极拳已经发展成为一项世界性的运动，传播到全球一百多个国家和地区，深受世界人民的喜爱。

一、太极拳名称的意蕴

太极拳运动创立于明末清初，迄今已有近四百年的历史。早期太极拳运动曾被称为"长拳""绵拳""十三势""软手"。至清朝乾隆年间，山西武术家王宗岳著《太极拳论》，用太极阴阳的哲理来解释太极拳，才确定了太极拳的名称。

"太极"一词出自《周易·系辞》，易有太极，是生两仪，"两仪"就是指"阴阳"。"阴阳"是古代哲学理论的代名词，用来说明一切事物内部不同属性的相互对立统一与转化。太极拳就是在符合阴阳对立统一的基础上，创造出的一套刚柔相济、内外相合、上下相通、快慢相兼、形意结合等阴阳相合的动作套路，它是综合性地继承和发展了明代在民间和军队中流行的各家拳法，结合了古代的导引术和吸纳术，吸取了古典唯物哲学、阴阳学说和中医基本理论的经络学说，成为一种内外兼修的拳种。

太极拳有五种步法，即：前进、后退、左顾、右盼、中定。劲法有八种，即：掤、捋、挤、按、採、挒、肘、靠，分配在东、南、西、北、东北、西北、东南、西南八个方向。八个手法与之前的五个步法合称叫十三势。

二、太极拳流派的形成

关于太极拳的创始,说法有多种,概括起来主要有许宣平创拳说、张三丰创拳说、王宗岳创拳说等。经诸多学者考证,最有说服力的是陈王廷创立了太极拳。

陈王廷是陈氏家族自山西迁至河南温县陈家沟的第九世后人,其父名抚民,祖名思贵,均好拳习武。《陈氏家谱》记载陈王廷是明末武庠生,清初文庠生。在山东称名手……陈氏拳手刀枪创始人。另据《温县志》记载,在明思宗崇祯十四年(1641),任温县乡兵守备,明亡后陷居家乡,晚年造拳自娱,教授弟子儿孙。

至陈氏十四世传人陈长兴(1771—1853)与陈有本(1780—1858)时,太极拳得到跨越式发展。陈长兴著有《太极拳十大要论》《太极拳用武要言》《太极拳战斗篇》等,并在祖传老架套路的基础上将太极拳套路由博归约,精炼归纳,创造性地发展成为现在的陈氏太极拳一路、二路(又叫炮锤),后人称其为太极拳老架(大架)。陈有本在太极拳原有套路基础上,逐渐舍弃了某些高难度和发劲动作,使其更加舒展大方,柔和自然,儒雅潇洒,收蓄兼并,发劲刚勇,也分为一路、二路,后人称为新架。

之后,随着太极拳影响的逐渐扩大和传播的日益广泛,习练太极拳的人也逐渐增多,自然而然地形成陈、杨、吴、武、孙等流派。如图1-1所示。

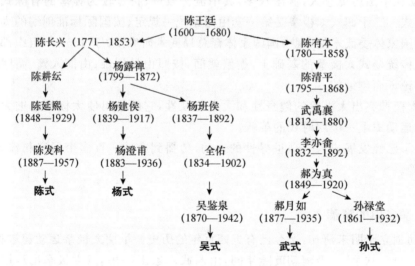

图1-1 太极拳流派形成简图

三、太极拳五大流派的特点

(一)陈式太极拳

陈式太极拳初创时有太极拳五路,炮锤一路,长拳108势一路。经五世传至陈长兴、陈有本这一代,原来108势长拳和太极拳(又叫十二势)第二至第五路已很少有人练习,陈氏拳家由博返约,专精练习第一路和炮锤。第一路以柔为主,柔中有刚,动作舒展大方,连绵贯穿,沉着稳健,一动无有不动,一静百骸相随;炮锤动作复杂,以刚为主,刚中有柔,动作急速、紧凑,套路中有蹿奔蹦跳、闪战腾挪的动作。

陈氏太极拳的特点可概括为：显刚隐柔，落点使刚，刚而紧，转换用柔，柔而弛，动作螺旋，忽隐忽现，蓄发并用，快慢相间，黏走助应，吞吐自然。

（二）杨式太极拳

杨露禅师从陈长兴学习陈氏老架太极拳，后又根据需要改编了拳套动作，传至其第三子杨建侯时修改为中架子，至杨澄甫时一再修订定型为大架子，成为目前流传最广的杨式太极拳。杨式太极拳的特点是速度较均匀，绵绵不断，动作简洁，运动似抽丝似的圆转，整个架式舒展和顺，结构严谨，中正圆满，轻灵沉着，浑厚庄重，平正朴实。练习时气派大，形象美，练法上由松入柔，刚柔相济。

（三）吴式太极拳

吴式太极拳是杨班侯之徒全佑（满族人）和他的儿子吴鉴泉父子俩在杨式太极拳所传小架基础上，逐步改进修润形成的一个流派。其特点是以柔化著称，动作轻松自然，连续不断，拳式小巧灵活。拳架由开展而紧凑，紧凑中不显拘谨。推手动作，立身中正，手法严密，着数多变，细腻绵柔，守静而不妄动，不乏机动灵活，黏走咸宜。

（四）武式太极拳

武禹襄师从杨露禅学习陈氏老架太极拳，又从陈清平学习新创套路，创造了武式太极拳。武式太极拳讲究练习时松静之中暗含开、合、隐、现。开则俱开，周身的骨节和肌肉群都微有开展的意思，开为发，发力的神意微现于体外。合则俱合，周身的骨节和肌肉群都微有收缩的意思。合为收，把运力的神意收隐于体内。武式在练功上是用内气的潜转和内劲的转换支配外形；左右手各管半个身体，不相逾越，出手不过脚尖。要求做到"外示安逸、内固精神"的由开到合，由合到开，互相转换的渐隐渐现。

（五）孙式太极拳

孙式太极拳是孙禄堂在武式太极拳、形意拳、八卦掌的基础上，参合三派之长而创的流派。它是一种架高步活的套路，动作小巧紧凑，重于收放开合，练习时要求进退相随，迈步必跟，退步必撤，动作圆活敏捷，每转身以开、合相接，所以又称为"开合活步太极拳"。

四、太极拳发展与传播

二十四式太极拳在1956年正式公布推广后，对国内外太极拳运动的普及和发展，起到了巨大的推动作用。

1978年，邓小平为日本友人题词"太极拳好"，使太极拳在世界产生了更广泛的影响，越来越多的海外宾朋到中国学习太极拳。

1982年，全国首届武术对抗项目散打、太极推手表演赛在北京举行，太极推手从此进入对抗性竞赛。

1986年，国家体委将太极拳、剑、推手列为全国正式比赛项目，并决定每年举行一次比赛。

1987年9月，在日本横滨举行的首届亚洲武术锦标赛上，太极拳作为正式比赛项目露面。

1988年4月，日本武术太极拳联盟组织日本百名太极拳爱好者到北京参加中日太极拳比赛交流大会。日本成为除中国以外开展太极拳运动最广泛的国家。

国际武术联合会 1990 年成立后，翌年举办首届世界武术锦标赛，将太极拳运动列为比赛项目。此后，各大洲举办的武术锦标赛中也都设立了太极拳项目。

1995 年 6 月，《全民健身计划纲要》颁布，太极拳成为练习人数最多的一项健身运动。

2000 年，国际武术联合会执委会会议通过决议，将每年的 5 月定为"世界太极拳月"，得到了各成员国家和地区的热烈响应，掀起了世界性的太极拳运动热潮。如今，二十四式太极拳已经成为一项享誉中外的体育运动。

二十四式太极拳简单易学、轻灵圆活，风格独特，老少皆宜，具有广泛的群众基础。长期习练可以提高身体的协调性、灵敏性和柔韧性，有助于身体各部位的均衡发展，改善神经系统机能，对心血管系统有良好的作用，符合上工治未病之理。因此，随着全民健身运动的蓬勃发展，太极拳已成为全民健身计划的重要组成部分。

第二节　太极拳特点与功用

一、太极拳的特点

1. 技术风格的丰富性

从太极拳的技术来看，目前流行的陈、杨、吴、武、孙五大流派的太极拳各具特色，技术风格各不相同。陈式太极拳的特点是缠丝旋转、顿足跳跃、松活弹抖；杨氏太极拳舒展大方、中正饱满、浑厚凝重；武式太极拳起承开合、节序清晰、法度严密；吴氏太极拳小巧玲珑、斜中寓正、川字步型、孙式太极拳架高步活、中正舒展、进退相随。二十四式简化太极拳由杨式太极拳简化而来，其特点如下。

（1）轻松柔和。

太极拳的架势比较平稳舒展，动作要求不僵不拘，符合人体运动的生理特征，而且，一般没有忽起忽落的明显变化和激烈的跳跃动作。所以，练习之后，虽然感到身上微微出汗，但很少发生气喘现象，给人以轻松愉快之感。不同年龄、性别和体质的人，都可以从事该项目的锻炼。

（2）连贯均匀。

整套太极拳动作，从"起势"到"收势"，不论动作的虚实变化和姿势的过渡转换，都是紧密衔接、连贯一气的，没有明显停顿的地方。太极拳强调"运动如抽丝"，整套动作速度均匀，前后连贯，好像行云流水，绵绵不断。

（3）圆活自然。

"圆活"是指动作变换自然而不停滞，表现在上肢处处带有弧形，保持空间的圆形、弧形、螺旋形或不同的曲线运行，避免直来直去，符合人体各关节自然弯曲状态。通过弧形活动进行锻炼，体现出动作的圆活自然和柔和的特点，使身体各部分得到均匀协调的发展。

（4）协调完整。

在太极拳运动中，不论是整个套路，还是单个动作，都要求上下相随，内（意念、呼吸）外

（躯干、四肢动作）一体，身体各部分之间要密切配合。打太极拳时，强调以腰为轴，要求上肢、下肢、躯干各部分协调配合运转，由脚而腿而腰一气完成，全身"一动无有不动"。以腰为轴，注重手脚的许多动作都是由躯干来带动，并且互相呼应，不要上下脱节或彼动此不动，显得呆滞脱节和支离破碎。

（5）虚实分明。

虚实分明是太极拳的主要特点。从动作整体看，一般是动作达到终点定式为"实"，动作变换过程为"虚"。从局部看，主要支撑体重的腿为"实"，辅助支撑或换步的腿为"虚"；体现动作主要内容的手臂为"实"，配合的手臂为"虚"。在劲力的变换中沉着、充实的动作为"实"，轻灵、含蓄的动作为"虚"。分清动作虚实，用力时就要有张有弛，区别对待。实的动作和部位用力要求沉着，虚的动作和部位要求轻灵、含蓄。

太极拳的动作，无论怎样复杂，首先要注意"中正安舒"的基本要求。凡是旋转的动作，应先把身体稳住再提腿换步；进退的动作，先落脚而后再慢慢改变重心。同时，做到沉肩、松腰、松胯以及手法上的虚实，也会有利于身体重心的稳定。

（6）呼吸自然。

练习太极拳时，由于动作轻松柔和，身体始终保持着缓和协调，所以初学太极拳的人，要注意保持自然呼吸。在做动作时，练习者按照自己的习惯和当时的需要进行呼吸，动作和呼吸不要互相约束。动作熟练之后，可根据个人锻炼体会的程度，毫不勉强地随着速度的快慢和动作幅度的大小，按照起吸落呼、开吸合呼的要求，使呼吸与动作自然配合。

（7）意识为先。

运用意识是太极拳的特殊锻炼方式。练习太极拳的全过程，要求用意识引导动作，把注意力贯注到动作之中去，在做每个动作时先想后做，随想随做，就是所谓的"神为主帅，身为驱使"和"意动身随"。要做到这一点，首先要保证练习时处于安静状态和集中注意力，因为这样才能有利于消除杂念，使心静体松，达到追求的意境。

2. 独特的技击性

太极拳首先是一种拳术，从它的起源来看，它是作为一种技击术发展而来的，只是它的运动特点比较适合大众健身而已。在动作演练上，它的技击性体现在每个动作的要求上，即使是作为健身手段练习，也应遵循其技术要求。如太极拳要求开裆圆胯，是为了有利于技击时下肢力量向上传递，如果做不到开裆圆胯在练习时容易产生"跪膝"现象，反而有损身体健康。同时，其技击性的独特性还表现在，太极拳一反常理地要求在技击时"用意不用力"，强调生理与心理的完美结合，突出反映了其"内外兼修"的特点，并且，太极拳在技击时反对"一力降十会"而是强调"以柔克刚""借力打力"，追求"后发先至""四两拨千斤"的技击效果，也正是这样的技击特点使得太极拳在一百多个拳种中独树一帜。

3. 健身价值的显著性

近年来，有学者研究表明，习练太极拳对改善心血管系统、呼吸系统、神经系统、免疫系统等人体各大系统的机能具有显著的效果。如刘玉萍（1996年）对简化二十四式太极拳的研究表明，老年人连续练习两套和三套太极拳后收缩压中等升高、很快恢复至运动前水平并随恢复期向后推移递减至正常人收缩压高度、舒张压在练习后降低与静态比有显著意义。

4. 鲜明的文化性

太极拳同其他拳种一样，孕育于中华民族的传统文化之中，是中华民族集体智慧的结晶。但是，太极拳从拳理到技术处处都与中国传统哲学紧密联系的特点却是其他拳种无法比拟的。太极拳的圆形运动要求和圆文化，以传统太极哲学为根源，而太极拳在技击上强调守静、反对主动进攻的防守策略，更是鲜明地体现了道家"尚柔、不争"的思想特点。此外，传统医学的导引吐纳之术被太极拳直接吸收，使得太极拳成为一种"形神兼备""内外若一""以意导动"的运动，强化了其健身性。

5. 广泛的适用性

太极拳轻柔缓慢的运动特点，使得各种人群都可以参与进来。特别是中老年人群，由于他们的生理机能正在退化，不适宜从事剧烈的运动，而太极拳正好符合中老年人的生理特点。并且太极拳在运动过程中要求虚实分明，从而形成了单腿承重的运动特点，这样可以使老年人下肢力量和平衡能力得到锻炼，可以有效防止老年人摔倒。而且，太极拳在动作上相对于其他拳术要简单，对习练者的要求比较低，几乎人人都可学习。此外，太极拳作为一种拳术，其技击性也吸引着大量的年轻人从事这项运动。其"以柔克刚"的技击特点，通过拆招推手的练习可以使身材瘦小的人获得转化进攻、避实就虚的能力，从而达到防身的目的。同时，我们也注意到一些企业开始要求员工习练太极拳，运用"太极哲学"来管理企业。这些无不说明，太极拳广泛的适用性。

二、太极拳的功用

1. 技击作用

太极拳作为"拳"，具有技击作用。太极拳具备完整的技术体系，包含着功法、套路、推手、散手。这一套"从功到用"的技术的存在是服务于技击的。太极拳同其他拳术存在一些共性的特征，如都是"功、套、用"三位一体，都有独特的劲法、都强调运用整体劲，都包含丰富的技法，等等。在当代，套路成为其主要的运动形式，但是传统的太极拳习练过程绝不仅仅是套路。杨澄甫曾说过"套路是体，推手是用"，这也说明，套路在传统太极拳中只是获得技击能力的一种训练手段。套路之后还有推手，通过推手的练习，可以让人在安全的条件下体验对抗的乐趣，也可以培养人们在随机条件下运用掤、捋、挤、按、采、挒、肘、靠八种劲法的能力，进而应用于散手对抗。

2. 健身作用

太极拳古谱中有"详推用意终何在，益寿延年不老春"的歌诀，这句话突出强调了太极拳的健身功能。大量的事实和科学实验也充分证明，太极拳是一项对身体十分有益的健身活动。太极拳结合传统医学的养生理论，强调"用意不用力"，呼吸细匀深长，运功时一动全动，腰为枢纽，从而达到提高神经系统、呼吸系统、运动系统等各系统机能的健身效果，此外，这些与"调心、调神、调息"的传统养生方法是相合的。科学研究也表明，长期练习太极拳对于预防心血管疾病、缓解失眠、抑郁、改善中老年人的呼吸功能、防止骨质疏松等具有显著的功效。

3. 陶冶情操，修身养性

太极拳在动作上要求柔和缓慢、舒展大方、虚实分明，在演练上讲究行云流水、连绵不绝，习练者在练习时通过优美的造型、流畅的动作，能够体验到传统文化中优雅、从容的美感。同时,太极拳的推手运动强调"后发先至""以柔克刚",可以培养人的谦虚礼让的优良品质。在练习太极拳的过程中,也可以获得人与人相处的道理、启发对人生的感悟,使练习者在锻炼身体的同时修养心性,获得生理机能与道德情操的统一,真正实现"术道并进",改善个人气质,通过太极拳的练习体悟人生的真谛。

第二章　太极拳知识与要点

本章主要介绍太极拳的基本知识和技术要领。习练太极拳讲究意、气、形、神——"意"即意识、意念，太极拳外形动作的锻炼和呼吸的锻炼，都是在意念的引导下进行的。练习太极拳要以"意"导"气"，呼吸深长细匀，通顺自然。对于运气的正确理解是"以气运身，务令顺遂，乃能便利从心"。"形"是指在太极拳练习中所采取的符合拳理要求的、正确的太极拳动作姿势。"神"主要指练习太极拳时的眼神与精神。练习太极拳不仅需要依法而行，领悟意、气、形、神的正确运用，还要熟悉身体部位的规范动作，如：虚灵顶劲竖项、沉肩坠肘坐腕、含胸拔背实腹、松腰敛臀圆裆。此外，本章还详尽地介绍了太极拳的九项基本技法要领，为了解和习练太极拳的人提供科学合理的技法说明和指导。

第一节　太极拳之意、气、形、神

一、意

习练太极拳讲究"凡此皆是意"。"意"即意念、意识，为思想的起点，行为的统帅。在太极拳的练习中，要求做到"以心行气，务令沉着，乃能收敛入骨""以气运身，务令顺遂，乃能便利从心""心为令，气为旗""以意导气、以气运身""用意不用力"等，强调意念在太极拳练习中始终居于主导地位。必须先有意，才有气的呼吸鼓荡和劲力的缠绕往复，才能主宰和支配肢体的运动。陈炎林先生在其《太极拳刀剑杆散手合编》一书中还专门就意气问题进行了论述"意即是心，心即是意。实则心与意，其间亦略有区别。心为意之主，意为心之副。心动则意起，意生则气随。"这些都强调了意念在太极拳中的重要性。太极拳外形动作的锻炼和呼吸的锻炼，都是在意念的引导下进行的。因此，为了收到较好的锻炼效果，在太极拳练习前，首先要做到排除杂念，集中注意力，处于一种心平气和的状态下，然后再全神贯注地不断用意识来引导每一个动作的完成。只有"心灵与意静，自然无处不轻灵"，只有"意气须换得灵，乃有圆活之趣"，把周身看成一个整体，将意识贯注于身体内外、上下、左右、前后，进而达到"表里粗精无处不到"的高度完整的境界，圆融精妙，"行住坐卧皆是太极"。另外，在太极拳的"用意"锻炼上，还应该强调意守的部位，也就是把注意力集中在身体的某一穴位上。如通常意守的穴位有"丹田""劳宫""命门"等穴位。这样，不仅可以更好地排除杂念，而且由于意守的穴位不同，可以调理身体内部气血的运行，改善脏腑的功能，起到防病治病的作用。

练习太极拳时，首先要做到"心静体松"才能达到"意注"的境界，才能做到更好地用"意"。"心静体松"是练习太极拳最主要的法则。它应贯穿于整个太极拳的练习过程中。所谓"心静"是指练拳时思想集中，抛开一切杂念，全神贯注于太极拳每一个细节动作的练习，肢体放松，以意念引导动作的变化和运行。这种"心静用意"引导动作的练拳方式，可以调节大脑皮层和中枢神经系统的机能，增强身体其他器官的功能。用意引导动作，可帮助精神集中，做到以意导体，意动形随，调节呼吸，使意识、动作和呼吸三者紧密结合，从而达到全面锻炼的目的。"体松"不是指全身的松懈和疲沓，而是要消除身体的拙力和肢体僵硬，按照动作的虚实变化，做到全身不该用力之处不用力，让全身关节、肌肉和内脏等达到最大限度的放松，做到形松意不松，逐步达到以松入柔，积柔成刚，刚柔相济。"体松"是练拳时姿态正确、周身协调、动作舒展、转换圆活及发劲的基础和保证，是身体"内外"协调的先决条件，只有"松"才能使动作协调，呼吸自然，思想安定。

二、气

在祖国医学中气的概念，一是指营养人体的精微物质，如水谷之气，呼吸之气等；二是指脏腑组织的活动能力，如：脾气、胃气、心气及经脉之气等。这两种含义之气，都充盈于全身的内外上下，推动着一切生理机能的正常运行。太极拳运动的特点，在于贵慢柔而养气。慢柔形于外，养气蕴于内。"气沉丹田""以意导气，以气运身"等，都反映了太极拳在练习中对"气"的特殊要求。例如习练太极拳时要求"遍体气流行，一定继续不能停"，说明任何动作都必须与呼吸相结合进行；而"行气如九曲珠，无微不到"则说明气的运行应该达到身体的任何部分，即使是身体的四梢（手指尖与脚趾尖），从而进入"呼吸通灵，周身罔间"的境界。但是，我们对于运气的正确理解是"以气运身，务令顺遂，乃能便利从心"，要以意导气，增大肺活量，而不是以力使气，强迫呼吸。由于太极拳的演练速度比较慢，因此在练习中更强调呼吸与动作的协调配合。在意识的调节下，把自身"内气"调动起来，通过不同的呼吸方式，主要使用腹部呼吸，用腹部的鼓荡变化来进行气的运转，所谓"腹内松净气腾然""气宜鼓荡"，使腹腔横膈膜对脏腑进行按摩，锻炼五脏六腑，改善其功能，使真气充沛并循经络运行，达到强身治病的目的。

练习太极拳要求呼吸深长细匀，通顺自然。根据太极拳练习者技术水平的高低，呼吸方法可分为自然呼吸、腹式顺呼吸、腹式逆呼吸和拳式呼吸。

自然呼吸：练习者在练拳时，呼吸方式不随拳式的变化而变化，完全顺其自然。多用于太极拳初学者。

腹式顺呼吸：是指吸气时腹部向外凸起，呼气时腹部自然内收的呼吸方式。

腹式逆呼吸：与腹式顺呼吸的刚好相反。吸气时腹部内收，呼气时腹部外凸。

拳式呼吸：是指呼吸随着拳式的变化而变化。

以上几种呼吸方法，不论采用哪种方法，都应自然、匀细、徐徐吐纳，与动作自然配合。对于初学者来讲，首选自然呼吸，保证动作不受呼吸的限制，呼吸同样不受动作的束缚。否则就容易产生憋气的现象。随着练习水平和个人体会程度的提高，可试着进行其他几种呼吸方式的运用。也可随着动作速度的快慢、幅度的大小，按照起吸落呼、开吸合呼、向前下按时呼和向后向上收时吸的原则逐步过渡到拳式呼吸。

三、形

太极拳要求习练者做到"形神兼备","神"是"形"的主宰,"形"是"神"的外化。具体地讲,"形"是指在太极拳练习中所采取的符合拳理要求的、正确的太极拳动作姿势,它是由许多具有不同技击和健身特色的形体动作所组成的。太极拳形的锻炼具有十分重要的意义,这是因为形的规格正确与否,直接影响着太极拳的锻炼质量和效果,因此拳谚有"势正气则顺,势错气则滞"的说法。在太极拳的练习中,通过形体的锻炼,运用身躯的旋转、缠绕,"以气运身",使气达于四肢,各部位动作协调一致,才能达到强壮身体,柔软筋骨的目的。对于形体的锻炼,我们通常采用单个动作和套路技术相结合的方式进行。在单个基本动作的练习中,练习者不仅要加深对每一个技术动作规格的了解,而且要逐步掌握动作与呼吸和意识的配合,为进行套路练习奠定基础。

太极拳讲究一动无有不动,始终以意念引导动作。每当一个动作完成时,意念中就有下一个动作出现,做到意连形随。整个套路练习从头到尾给人一种连贯圆活的感觉,如行云流水。太极拳是缓慢匀速的运动,在意念领先的前提下,通过不断练习,达到势势意连形随的境地。

太极拳练习者若要更好地演绎"形",则要求周身协调。连贯圆活是衡量一个人太极拳功夫深浅的主要依据。有"一动无有不动,一静无有不静"之说。"连贯"一是指肢体的连贯,即"节节贯穿"。要求以腰为枢纽,对于下肢应该做到以腰带胯,以胯带膝,以膝带足的节节带动和环环相扣。对于上肢则要做到以腰带背,以背带肩,以肩带肘,以肘带手的连贯带动和环环相扣。二是指动作与动作间的衔接,即"势势相连"。表明前一式的结束就是下一式的开始,势势之间没有停顿和间断。圆活是指动作圆满活顺自然。要求身体的每个部位都呈弧形,每个动作的手法、步法、身法的运动路线呈弧形。整个动作过程做由内及外的弧线运动。所以也把身体在运动中的状态形容为身体如"五张弓"。即两臂,两腿和躯干,在运动过程中始终保持弧形。

四、神

这里的"神"主要指练习太极拳时的眼神与精神。"手、眼、身、法、步"是拳术的五个锻炼要点,所以眼神与动作的配合对提高整个练习的效果很重要。同样,练习者的精神状态和精神面貌也反映自己对动作的理解和把握,如对内要气宜鼓荡,对外要外示安逸、面容自然等,表现出沉着、舒展、自然的神气。

太极拳是一种轻灵、缓慢、沉稳的拳术,动作如抽丝,迈步如猫行。太极拳以阴阳转换理论为指导,在每一势和每一动中,始终有着阴阳转换,即虚与实的转换。动作的虚实转换不但要互相渗透,还需在意识指导下变换灵活,达到"无一处无虚实,无一处无变化"的状态。太极拳练习过程中的"神",即随着太极拳轻灵、沉稳、虚涵等要求不断地在练习中转换和变化,始终使身心内外协调完整,达到统一和谐的境地。

总之,练拳时必须舌抵上腭,唇齿相合,自然呼吸,身体中正,含胸拔背,沉肩坠肘,头正顶悬,裹裆收臀,上下成一直线,落步分清虚实,处处力求圆满,周身轻灵,眼随手走,呼吸自然,上下左右相系,无思无虑,达到心平气和的境界。而沉气松力,须时刻注意,气沉则呼吸调和,力松则拙力消除。每势都要求外面形式顺,内部舒适不强硬。才能胸膈开展,气血调和,对于身心才有很大功益。如果姿势做得不正确,违背练拳要领,则气滞胸膈,浮而不定,非但不能从太极拳的练习中得到益处,反而会导致疾病由此产生。只有集特殊的技击性、突出的哲理性、明显的健身性于一体,并符合太极拳一系列技术要求,才算是有益的太极拳,好的太极拳。

第二节　练习太极拳对身体部位的要求

一、头部

虚灵顶劲竖项

练习太极拳时,对头部姿势的要求是自然上顶,避免颈部肌肉硬直,不要东偏西歪或自由摇晃。头颈动作应随着身体位置和方向的变换,与躯干的旋转上下连贯协调一致。面部要自然,下颏向里收回,用鼻呼吸。口自然合闭。

眼神要随着身体的转动,注视前手(个别时候看后手)或平视前方,神态力求自然,注意力一定要集中,否则会影响锻炼效果。

经络学说有以头为百脉之宗的说法。头部虚灵上顶,好像有一股气要向上顶出,又好似头顶上有绳索悬着,使其平正而不倾斜,下颌内含,颈部松直自然而不僵硬。虚灵顶劲可使头部自然垂直,有利于练拳时的控制平衡和中枢神经对器官机能的调节等。

"满身轻灵顶头悬"。灵机于顶,不仅能使全身轻灵活泼,免除重滞,而且是身心合一,内外兼修,是精神与躯体相结合的关键。要保持虚灵顶劲的姿势,颈部要不松塌和不僵硬,端正竖起,颈项的自然放松竖起能使头部左右转动时自然灵活,达到头正、顶平。只有头部端正才能使身体姿势表现得更好。做到虚灵顶劲,才能精神饱满、意会贯注,保持练习时的动作沉稳和扎实。

二、躯干

含胸拔背实腹

含胸是胸部含而不露,既不能故意内凹,也不应该挺胸外凸;拔背是指当胸向内微含时,两肩中间脊骨顶微向外鼓起,背阔肌稍微向上提,使"牵动往来,气贴背,敛入脊骨",使背部肌肉产生一定张力和弹性,以便于行气运招。太极拳的含胸拔背是一种身体基本姿势要求。进行太极拳练习时,练习者含胸拔背的姿态既能使胸腔上下径拉长,横膈肌有更大向下舒展余地,有利于腹式呼吸的深长,吸入更多的氧气,又能有助于身体重心的下沉。

横膈肌运动所产生的腹式呼吸,使腹部肌肉逐步得到锻炼,腹部渐渐充实圆满,尤其是下腹部的充实,更有益于气沉丹田的要求。腹部随练习会时松弛时紧张,但始终保持松静的状态和感觉。含胸拔背实腹相互作用,练拳时保持着躯干的基本姿势。

太极拳要领中指出要"含胸拔背",或者"含蓄在胸,运动在两肩",意思是说在锻炼过程要避免胸部外挺,但也不要过分内缩,应顺其自然。"含胸拔背"是互相联系的,背部肌肉随着两臂伸展动作，尽量地舒展开，同时注意胸部肌肉要自然放松，不可使其紧张，这样胸就有了"含"的意思，背也有"拔"的形式，从而也可免除胸肋间的紧张，呼吸调节也自然了。

三、腰臀

松腰敛臀圆裆

练习太极拳，要求身体端正安舒。要做到这点，腰部起着重要的作用。在流传的说法中有"腰脊为第一主宰""刻刻留心在腰间""腰为车轴"等。这都说明腰是身体转动的关键，对全身动作的变化、调整和稳定重心，起着非常重要的作用。练习时，无论进退或旋转，凡是由虚而逐渐落实的动作，腰部都要有意识地向下松垂，以助气下沉。腰部下垂时，注意要端正安舒，腰腹部不可前挺或后屈，以免影响转换时的灵活性。腰部向下松垂，还可以增加两腿力量，稳固底盘，使得动作圆活、完整。腰是身体转动的关键部位，是四肢运动的中轴，关系到全身平衡的调整与内劲的运转，所以要做到"活泼于腰""刻刻留心在腰间""命意源头在腰际"。练习时，对腰部的要求是松而沉，也只有腰坐到松沉，才能达到"腰如弓把"，腰部灵活没有僵劲，才能更有弹性和爆发力，便于用意。要做到腰部松沉，要调整脊柱与骨盆的相对位置，做到腰部竖直，以满足"尾闾中正神贯顶"的要求。松腰并不是说腰部完全松软无力，而是有意识控制下的"松"，就是腰部没有僵劲。太极拳套路练习中，如搂膝拗步动作向前迈步时必须松腰，搬拦锤、闪通臂、单鞭等动作中，拳或掌向前伸出时，必须松腰。

敛臀是在松腰的基础上使臀部稍做内收，同时和含胸拔背相互协调配合，使身体的脊背成自然的弧形。敛臀时，放松臀部和腰部肌肉，使臀部肌肉向外下方舒展，然后向前、向内收敛，好似臀部把小腹托起，有利于气沉丹田的要求。

当两胯撑开，两膝有微向里扣的感觉时，就能起到圆裆的作用。胯关节是协调腰腿动作的主要关节，如果胯关节紧张，腰腿就很难相顺相随。圆裆和松胯相配合能使腰部灵活、起到臀部内敛的作用。

练习太极拳时要求敛臀，保持自然状态，避免臀凸出或左右扭动。要松腰、正脊以维持躯干的正直。总之，动作时，臀部始终要保持一定的弧度，推掌、收掌动作都不要突然断劲，这样才能做到既有节分又能连绵不断，轻而不浮，沉而不僵，灵活自然。

四、肩肘

沉肩坠肘坐腕

太极拳的手臂一伸一屈都不可平出平入，直来直往，应把腕部和前臂的旋转动作确切地表现出来，凡是收掌动作，手掌应微微含蓄，但不可软化、飘浮。出掌要自然，手指要舒展，拳要松握，不要太用力。

手和肩的动作是完整一致的。如果手过度向前引伸，就容易把臂伸直，达不到"沉肩垂肘"的要求；而过分地沉肩垂肘，忽略了手的向前引伸，又容易使臂部过于弯曲。

人体上肢的三大关节为肩关节、肘关节和腕关节。练习太极拳时在松肩的前提下要求沉肩坠肘，沉肩坠肘有利于躯干的含胸拔背，同时会有身体重心下沉的内劲感觉。沉肩是使肩松活而下沉，两臂能有灵活自然运转的余地。坠肘是肘尖时常取向下之意，肘松而下坠，劲力内含，有助于沉气，既能护肋，又可以增加手臂伸引、回缩的力量。

坐腕（塌腕）是腕关节向手背一侧自然屈起，无论在定势动作和运转动作中都须注意坐腕要求。坐腕对各类手法的劲力都有积极作用，如腕部松懈则前臂无力。掌握自然伸展的舒指与坐腕相配合，既有动作形象美感，又有臂部的劲力体现。

五、腰腿

松腰、松胯、屈膝

在练习太极拳的过程中，对于步法的进退变换和周身的稳定程度，两腿起着决定性作用。因此要求腿部动作要正确、灵活、稳当。在练习时，要特别注意重心移动、脚放的位置、腿弯曲的程度、重心的移动和两腿的虚实变化以及整个套路动作的前后衔接。

腿部活动时，总的要求是松胯、屈膝、两脚轻起轻落，使下肢动作轻、稳、进退灵便。迈步时，一腿支撑体重，稳定重心；然后另一腿缓缓迈出。脚的起落，要轻巧灵活。前进时，脚跟先着地；后退时，脚掌先着地，然后慢慢踏实。横步时，侧出腿先落脚尖，然后脚掌、脚跟依次落地。跟步、垫步都是先落脚尖或脚掌。

步型和步法都要求腿部动作虚实分明，除"起势""收势"外，避免体重同时落在两脚上（双重）。右腿支撑大部分体重时，则右腿为实，左腿为虚；左腿支撑大部分体重时，则左腿为实，右腿为虚。为了维持身体平衡，虚脚起着一个支点作用（如虚步的前脚和弓步的后脚）。蹬脚、分脚的动作，宜慢不宜快（个别动作除外），应保持身体平衡稳定。

第三节 太极拳基本技法要领

一、上下相随

在进行太极拳练习的时候，不论做哪一个动作都要使上肢、下肢、躯干等各部分做协调的运转，这种协调运转就叫作上下相随。太极拳理论认为："其根在脚，发于腿，主宰于腰，形于手指，由脚而腿而腰总需完整一气。"这句话的意思是说当我们在练习太极拳的时候，练习者的脚就好像植物的根一样，可以使身体稳固，而这种稳固要由腿部肌肉收缩发力来完成，此力一直灌注到脚跟下，对地面产生作用力；腰是整个身体的主宰，是身体力量上传下达的枢纽；由腰发出的劲力，向下通过腿传达到脚，向上可以通过肩和臂灌达手指。因此，在完成太极拳任何一个动作的过程中，都要使全身气力完整，一气呵成，使人体通过脚与地面产生的反作用力以一个整体表达出来，这样才能做到上下相随。

太极拳理论中又有："……向前退后，乃能得机得势，由不得机得势处，身便散乱……"意思是说，上下相随，可以使动作的进退得机得势，由此产生的结果是身法不至于散乱。因此，上下相随的意义可以从以下两方面进行把握。

第一，就运动意义而言，太极拳运动可以促进身体的全面发展，它不是单独锻炼身体的某一部分，而是使整个身体，包括内脏器官系统，都通过四肢和躯干的上下相随和完整协调的活动而得到全面锻炼。

第二，就太极拳的技击意义来说，必须达到上下相随才能做到得机得势，身法必须完整一气,掌握主动权,进退得宜,才能克敌制胜。所谓"上下相随人难进",就是强调上下相随在太极拳攻防技击中的重要性,如果身法散乱,手脚不能很好配合,那一定会露出破绽,则容易被人克制。

在练习的过程中,要做到上下相随应该注意以下三点。

第一,在练习太极拳时,不论哪一个动作,都要使手脚动作协调一致,不能出现先运动脚、后运动手或者先动手、后动脚的先后之分。一般练习者最容易犯的毛病是脚先到手后到,即迈步较快,手势较慢;或手先到,脚未到。

第二,练习太极拳时,出现屈腿、坐腰等动作不能随身体一齐运动的情况。这些毛病的根源往往在腰腿上,克服缺点也要从腰腿部开始,发现以后,立即纠正,时时注意能做到上下相随。例如,倒卷肱,右手向回收缩时左脚也要同时撤回,右脚向后撤回,左手同时向前推出,做到上下相随。同时,强调以腰为轴,初学者尤应注意两脚保持一定的横向距离和适当的前后距离,实现灵活转动。

第三,通过太极推手能进一步练习和体验上下相随。例如,两个人做活步推手时要求手法和步法一致,进步则挤,退步则捋,不能有丝毫迟缓,否则就容易被人制约。

二、内外相合

"内"是指五脏六腑及其机能,特别是大脑及其所产生的机能——精神、心理、意识。身体的一切活动是在神经系统,特别是在高级神经系统——大脑皮层的支配下形成的,当脑兴奋时,人就显得精神饱满;脑在抑制时,人就显得精神萎靡。练习太极拳时要求内外相合,就是要求脑包括内脏系统机能水平达到与身体运动相匹配的最佳状态。

"外"泛指身体的四肢百骸。身体的全部或局部活动,即使是最微小的活动都是在神经系统的支配下完成的。太极拳理论认为:"神为主帅,身为驱使",在神经系统的统一指挥下,精神和肉体的运动紧密结合在一起,合而为一,达到"内外相合"。在精神沉静下来,身心松弛安舒的状态下,动作柔和稳健、活泼轻灵、随意挥洒如行云流水般的运动,可以使人神清气爽,身心得到极大程度的放松,从而促进人体健康,起到保健治病的作用。

三、中正安舒

中正安舒是指在练习太极拳时,要使躯干保持自然舒展,不偏不倚的状态。"无使有凸凹处;无使有缺陷处",就是要求在练习太极拳时不能使关节处于僵硬不灵活的状态,不能使腰腿的方向和脚的落点方向不顺当,致使身体觉得别扭不自然。中正安舒对人体健康影响很大。进行太极拳练习时一定不要使肌肉、关节紧张,只有使其放松才能使胸腔扩张,肺脏舒展,更好地促进气血流通。练习时注意保持尾闾中正,就会防止躯干的前俯后仰、左右歪斜。否则,动作既不优美,呼吸也不自然舒畅,身体也容易失去平衡,重心不易掌握,推手时往往处于被动局面。

四、轻灵沉稳

轻灵是太极拳主要特点之一。所谓"轻灵",是指全身肌肉和关节都要放松,心神也要稳定,一招一式都要用意不用力,圆转灵活。

在从事锻炼时,如果使肌肉、关节放松,达到轻灵,则能使周身气血通畅,同时也便于用意念引导动作,使气血按照动作的要求而运转,长期坚持,就会产生良好的锻炼效果。相反,如果肌肉紧张时,全身筋脉也会随之紧张,不利于血液循环。从技击含义讲,轻灵使人肌肉放松,肢体不僵滞,反应速度和动作速度加快,爆发力增加而不产生拙劲。

沉稳,就是指在练习太极拳时精神要沉着镇定,动作稳当踏实。沉稳是在精神稳定、全身放松的状态下练成的。

初学太极拳者做到轻灵沉稳要求精神不紧张,要求放松,每一动作都遵守"用意不用力"的要点,动作配合呼吸,吸气时有助于发展轻灵,呼气时有助于发展沉稳。

五、刚柔相济

太极拳的刚和柔是相互依存和相互转化的,刚中寓柔,柔中有刚。进行太极拳练习时,应保证动作中该收缩的肌群达到从听从意念支配到有控制地收缩的转变,同时对抗肌又协调放松,刚柔此时很接近于虚实。柔近于虚,刚近于实。动作虚实经过一段时间的练习,可以使身体各部分练成似松非松、轻沉兼备、刚柔内含的状态,既有坚实的刚劲,又富于弹性和韧性的柔劲,极轻灵而又极稳重,极柔软而又极坚刚。在动作的同一瞬间,刚柔的比例并不同等。由动作的整体看,偏重于柔的时间多于刚的时间,每势的运转过程轻松柔和,定势的刹那间才偏于刚劲。对有显于外的刚性发劲,练习时不能用全力,应该循序渐进,逐渐提高。如果发现增加发力时感到生硬,失去弹性,没有圆活、顺畅的感觉,说明刚有余而柔不足,需要及时调整。

以健身治病为目的的太极拳练习,必须偏重于轻柔。在精神镇定、集中的状态下,使肌肉关节放松,气血通畅,以意念支配动作,长久坚持自然有利于健康。

六、虚实与双重

虚就是灵活、松软,实就是紧张、坚实的意思。虚实在太极拳运动中相辅相成,相反相成,对立统一。以下肢为例,左腿负担全身的重量或大部分体重则左腿为实,右腿为虚;如果是右腿负担全身或大部分体重则右腿为实,左腿为虚。对于双手的虚实而言,意念着重于哪一只手则哪一只手就为实,另一只手为虚。

人体各部位虚实的存在,按位置相对而言不是固定不变的,应该随着拳术姿势的变化而变化,虚实都只是暂时的。王宗岳的《太极拳论》中说:"左重则左虚,右重则右杳,仰之则弥高,俯之则弥深",即虚中有实,实中有虚,做到这几点的关键在于运用虚实变化,要求在虚实动作中肌肉的张弛有意识地留有少许伸缩的弹性,以便关节肌肉伸缩转化。对实的用劲要注意分寸,既不滞涩,也不是僵硬不灵。例如,单鞭,左手为实,右手为虚。实中有虚,就是注意力集中在左手,而不该用力的部位都要放松。太极拳对身体协调性的要求较高,只有当肌肉没有多余的紧张时,动作才能完成得轻松自如,柔和连贯。若肌肉参与工作不及时或对抗肌放松较迟,动作就会变得生硬,不但影响肌肉的工作能力,而且影响动作完成的准确性。

对太极拳虚实的掌握和运用,要做到:① 在每一动作中,首先分清楚下肢的虚实,经常变换用一腿负担体重,可以逐渐增强下肢力量。② 迈步不要过大、过远,如果两脚间距离过远,则换步不灵,虚实不易变化。③ 身体中正不偏,学会用意不用力,一足落地踏稳再迈另一步。

太极拳理论中有双重则滞的说法,"双重"指两手两足向同一方向发出紧张僵硬之力的动作状态。《太极轻重浮沉解》中也明确谈到"双重为病,失于填实","填实"即形容实中丧失弹性,属于失掉灵活的僵力,是不符合太极拳习练要求的。例如,"马步"两脚相距过宽,下蹲太过,失掉弹性劲而影响动作灵活时就犯了"双重"的错误;再如弓步,如果两脚前后距离过长,屈膝膝关节超过足尖也会出现"双重"。

总之,在太极拳练习过程中,凡是不利于肌肉张弛变换,影响动作灵活协调,发劲用力失去弹性的,都要避免。

七、推手与懂劲

推手是运用太极拳中掤、捋、挤、按、采、挒、肘、靠等方法进行的双人练习。推手是一种对抗性练习,可以增进练习者的兴趣,增强实战能力。"懂劲"就是通过推手增强人的感知觉能力,推手练习达到一定水平后,对方的手或者身体的某一部分与自己的身体接触时就立即能感知到其用力的轻重虚实,并随之应对,用正确的用力方式化解处理,使自己占据主动地位。达到懂劲的程度,太极推手就会愈练愈静,进步快,效果好,招法运用自如。

八、用意不用力

练习太极拳时,要求精神贯注而肌肉不要紧张,通常理解为用意不用力。意就是指意念、意识、心意等,在太极拳中指用意念、意识等指导自己的行动。

力是由人体肌肉收缩运动而产生的。力量产生的大小,除了与人体肌肉组织有关系,还与大脑皮层的兴奋性和神经系统的灵活性有很大关系,尤其是爆发力更是如此。太极拳的动作在意识引导下进行,即在大脑的支配下活动,用意不用力,对改进神经系统机能有良好的作用。由于太极拳的某些动作比较复杂,需要大脑在紧张的活动下完成这些动作,间接对中枢神经系统起到训练作用,同时也促进其他系统、器官的机能活动。由于不用拙力而使身体处于放松状态,也有利于血液循环,使机体氧和营养物质的输送效率提升。长期坚持,有利于促进身体健康。

用意不用力强调动作、劲力在意念的控制下能收能放,做到随心所欲,当需要发力用劲时一触即发。练习太极拳时,做任何动作都不用拙力,动作要圆活松软;出拳时,拳头不能握紧而要拳心虚空,不能用猛劲;用脚时,将腿轻轻提起,徐徐蹬出,不用力不求直,精神贯注于手和脚,则意念也在手和脚上,做到意动身随。

九、粘黏连随

所谓粘、黏、连、随,就是太极推手时应该遵循的要点。即在推手时,个人的手臂与对方的手臂永远保持恰如其分的接触,不论动作怎样变化都不使之离开。

粘:就是提高拔上的意思。当和对方搭手时,要凭借个人推手技术向上引起对方的手臂,使其身体上重下轻,重心不稳,甚至使其足跟离地,目的在于将对方发出。

黏:无论对方手法与身法怎样变化,想方设法使自己的手臂永不离开对方的手臂,像黏在一起似的。

连：推手时，有意识地使自己的力量与对方的力量连接起来，以便更加深入地了解对方力量的大小和来龙去脉。

随：依据对方的动作，缓急相随，进退相依。只要与对方搭上手，就不能使之轻易脱开，不论对方想怎样摆脱，自己的手都要紧跟上去，这是取胜的最好时机。

在推手的初级阶段，没有发展到懂劲的程度，会出现丢、顶的毛病。丢，就是与对方脱离接触。顶，就是与对方的劲力发生顶牛现象。在练习时，要想做好粘、黏、连、随和不丢、不顶，需要坚持用意不用力，要根据对方的情况随势而动。不仅两手，而且身法、步法都要上下相随、周身协调地共进退，做到形要连，意也要连，彼进我退，彼退我进，彼沉我松，利用身体的感知觉能力感知对方力量的大小、方向，把握时机，占据主动。

十、掤、捋、挤、按、采、挒、肘、靠

太极推手的动作共有八种：掤、捋、挤、按、采、挒、肘、靠，通常把前四种称为四正推手法，后四种称为四隅推手法。

掤，就是向上托的意思，在搭手时，逆着对方之劲承而向上，使对方之劲不得下降，如果运用得好，可以使对方被掀起。杨氏太极拳八法秘诀中关于"掤"的表述为：

掤劲义何解　如水负行舟　先实丹田气　次要顶头悬
全体弹簧力　开合一定间　任有千斤重　飘浮亦不难

捋，与对方搭手时，凡是对方用掤或挤的技法时，向后下方顺势用力，如果运用得好，可以使对方向前倾倒。杨氏太极拳八法秘诀中关于"捋"的表述为：

捋劲义何解　引导使之前　顺其来势力　轻灵不丢顶
力尽自然空　丢击任自然　重心自维持　莫为他人乘

挤，搭手时，以手或臂等部分直接往对方身上用力，或者往对方身上推，使之无法动弹，然后将对方挤出去。杨氏太极拳八法秘诀中关于"挤"的表述为：

挤劲义何解　用时有两方　直接单纯意　迎合一动中
间接反应力　如球撞壁还　又如钱投鼓　跃然击铿锵

按，在实践中，凡是遇到对方挤我时即用手下按，以破前挤之势。杨氏太极拳八法秘诀中关于"按"的表述为：

按劲义何解　运用如水行　柔中寓刚强　急流势难当
遇高则膨满　逢洼向下潜　波浪有起伏　有孔无不入

采，在搭手时，凡是能制着对方，并采彼之力近彼之身这为采。善于用采者，不管对方用怎样的力度进攻，都可以用"采"化解掉。杨氏太极拳八法秘诀中关于"采"的表述为：

采劲义何解　如权之引衡　任尔力巨细　权后知轻重
转移只四两　千斤亦可平　若问理何在　杠杆之作用

挒，就是扭转的意思，凡是转移化解对方之力而进攻其身者，都叫挒。挒的力学原理是使对方之力分解，再由侧方进攻。杨氏太极拳八法秘诀中关于"挒"的表述为：

挒劲义何解　旋转若飞轮　投物于其上　脱然掷丈寻
君不见漩涡　卷浪若螺纹　落叶堕其上　倏尔便沉沦

肘，就是指肘关节，在实践中用肘关节攻防。杨氏太极拳八法秘诀中关于"肘"的表述为：

  肘劲义何解　方法有五行　阴阳分上下　虚实须辨清
  连环势莫当　开花捶更凶　六劲融通后　运用始无穷

靠，凡是用肩和背的外侧攻击对手的技法就是"靠"，"靠"一定要在接近对手身体并且处于最合适的机会时运用，不能轻易使用。杨氏太极拳八法秘诀中关于"靠"的表述为：

  靠劲义何解　其法分肩背　斜飞势用肩　肩中还有背
  一旦得机势　轰然如捣碓　仔细维重心　失中徒无功

第三章 太极拳基础动作及要领

本章以图文并茂的方式生动详细地介绍了太极拳的基础动作及要领。太极拳的基础动作既可以是相对独立单个动作,也可以是几个动作的组合。太极拳的基础动作包括手型、手法、步型、步法等。根据不同的手型、手法、步型、步法、身法、腿法以及跳跃、平衡等组成各种动作练习,如运臂练习、行步练习和推手练习。通过基础动作练习,不仅能规范地掌握太极拳的形态和完成方法,而且还能更好地提高动作的协调性和技巧性,为以后完成套路练习打下扎实基础。

第一节 基础动作

一、手型

太极拳的基本手型包括拳、掌和勾等。

（一）拳

1. 动作方法

食指、中指、无名指与小指四指自然卷握,拇指压于中指和食指的第二关节上。如图3-1所示。

2. 技术要点

拳要松握,拳心虚空。

3. 错误纠正

练习时易出现拳头紧握,动作僵硬不柔和等问题。因此,应了解把握太极拳练习时对身体各部位的要求,不刻意用力,强调自然和谐。

（二）掌

1. 动作方法

五指微曲分开,掌心微含,虎口撑圆,手指不可僵直或过分弯曲。如图3-2所示。

2. 技术要点

掌指放松,顺其自然。

3. 错误纠正

练习时易出现掌心刻意外挺造成手掌、手指和小臂肌肉紧张,动作僵硬等问题,应注意掌指的适度放松。

（三）勾

1. 动作方法

五指第一关节捏拢在一起，屈腕，用力自然，不要太紧张。如图3-3所示。

2. 技术要点

五指捏拢，适度屈腕。

3. 错误纠正

练习时易出现手腕放松、屈腕不够或过度屈腕造成手和手臂紧张等问题，应该反复练习加以体会。

图3-1

图3-2

图3-3

二、手法

太极拳的手法分为掤、捋、挤、按、采、挒、肘、靠、冲拳、贯拳、分掌、抱掌、撑掌、穿掌、架掌和云手。这里主要介绍最基本的几种手法。

（一）掤

1. 动作方法

左（右）手臂成弧形，由下向前上掤架，掌高与肩平，掌心向内，前臂外侧为力点，右（左）手按于右（左）胯旁，掌心向下，指尖向前。如图3-4、图3-5所示。

图 3-4　　　　　　　　　　　图 3-5

2. 技术要点

身体中正,眼随手走,用意不用力,周身协调。

3. 错误纠正

练习时前臂故意发力破坏身体平衡,注意在放松的状态下用意识去指导动作的完成。

（二）捋

1. 动作方法

两臂微屈,掌心斜相对,双掌随腰转动由前向后划弧捋至身体侧后方。如图 3-6、图 3-7 所示。

图 3-6　　　　　　　　　　　图 3-7

2. 技术要点

身体中正,腰为主宰转动用力。

3. 错误纠正

练习中常出现身体前俯单纯靠两手臂用力的错误,应该时刻提醒初学者注意腰部的转动,以腰带臂用力。

（三）挤

1. 动作方法

前手臂屈肘直腕,后手坐腕贴近前手小臂内侧,两臂同时向前挤出。挤出时两臂撑圆,高不过肩,低不过胸。如图3-8、图3-9所示。

图 3-8

图 3-9

2. 技术要点

前挤时注意拧腰,身体重心前移成弓步,上下肢动作协调一致。

3. 错误纠正

初学者在练习时会出现双臂前挤到位而下肢弓步未完成,身体重心继续前移的现象;或者是下肢弓步到位,而双臂仍然向前挤得不协调现象。出现这些问题有多方面的原因,主要是由于身体动作不协调造成,平时应该多加强身体协调性的练习。

（四）按

1. 动作方法

两手掌同时由后向前推按,指尖向上,掌心向前,双臂微屈,肘部松沉,与胸同高。如图3-10、图3-11所示。

2. 技术要点

按掌时注意腰、腿用力协调一致,动作定势时注意沉肩垂肘。

3. 错误纠正

初学者的易犯错误与挤的动作相似,平时应多注意身体协调性练习加以纠正。

图 3-10

图 3-11

（五）冲拳

1. 动作方法

拳从腰间旋转向前打出成立拳，拳眼向上，臂微屈。如图 3-12、图 3-13 所示。

图 3-12

图 3-13

2. 技术要点

出拳时蹬地拧腰，协调用力，力达拳面。

3. 错误纠正

初学者练习时会出现握拳较紧，冲拳后肘关节伸直且僵硬，肩部前送且耸起的情况。所以，练习中应多强调对身体各部位的控制来加以纠正错误动作。

（六）贯拳

1. 动作方法

双手握拳从身体两侧下方向前上方弧形横打，双臂微屈撑圆，拳眼斜向下，力点在拳面。如图 3-14、图 3-15 所示。

图 3-14

图 3-15

2. 技术要点

双拳弧形向前击打，力达拳面，两拳间距离约同头宽。

3. 错误纠正

在做贯拳练习时，初学者经常会出现定势时双肩向前上提拉从而形成耸肩缩脖的错误，练习时应强调沉肩垂肘的要求，以纠正错误动作。

（七）推掌

1. 动作方法

掌从胸前向前推出，掌心向前，指尖向上，与胸同高，手臂微屈。如图 3-16、图 3-17 所示。

图 3-16

图 3-17

2. 技术要点

掌心虚含,沉肩坠肘,动作协调。

3. 错误纠正

推掌时掌心过分外挺,动作僵硬不柔和,平时应多做在意念指导下的动作练习,以纠正错误动作。

（八）抱掌

1. 动作方法

两掌在身体两侧立掌,掌心向外,由身体两侧向前划弧合抱于胸前,双手交叉,掌心向后。如图 3-18、图 3-19 所示。

图 3-18

图 3-19

2. 技术要点

动作自然,注意松肩垂肘,身体中正。

3. 错误纠正

初学者练习此动作时往往会出现双掌由体侧向胸前合抱时上体前俯、耸肩的问题,平时练习时可以对着镜子或与同伴相互帮助进行。

（九）分掌

1. 动作方法

两手在胸前交叉合抱,向左右两侧分举,掌心均向外,指尖向上,手腕与肩同高。如图 3-20、图 3-21 所示。

2. 技术要点

动作自然协调,两掌在向身体两侧分举的过程中完成外翻动作。

3. 错误纠正

初练者在练习此动作时会出现两掌高于头部向外分举,从而造成耸肩,身体紧张等问题。在平时练习时应多注意分掌时高度不要高于脸部。

图 3-20

图 3-21

三、步型

太极拳的基本步型分为弓步、虚步、独立步、仆步,等等。

(一) 弓步

1. 动作方法

弓步时两脚脚掌均全部着地,前腿屈膝大腿接近水平,膝部与脚尖垂直,方向一致。后腿不能完全蹬直,后脚尖内扣斜向前方 45 度,两脚横向距离约 30~40 厘米。左腿在前屈膝为左前弓步,右腿在前为右前弓步。如图 3-22 所示。

图 3-22

2. 技术要点

上体中正不偏不倚，前腿屈曲大腿接近水平，承担约六成体重，后腿承担约四成体重。

3. 错误纠正

最常见的错误是做弓步时两脚没有一定的横向距离，易造成身体稳定性差，失去平衡。练习时应该注意两脚间有一定的横向距离，增加身体的稳定性。

（二）虚步

1. 动作方法

后腿屈蹲，脚跟与臀部基本垂直，脚尖稍向外展，全脚掌着地；前腿微屈，膝关节略上提，前脚掌或脚跟轻轻点地。如图 3-23、图 3-24 所示。

图 3-23

图 3-24

2. 技术要点

身体中正，重心平稳，虚实分明。

3. 错误纠正

虚步时点地的脚几乎不承担身体的重量，练习时容易出现身体重心不稳的问题。初学者可以先由两脚共同分担体重，然后逐渐减少点地脚承担体重的比例。

（三）独立步

1. 动作方法

支撑腿微屈站立，另一腿屈膝上提高于腰部，脚尖向下；上体保持正直。如图 3-25 所示。

2. 技术要点

身体中正，重心平稳，上提腿膝关节尽量向上，小腿及踝关节适当放松。

3. 错误纠正

初学者往往出现重心不稳、上提腿脚尖勾屈等问题。平时应该多做控制身体姿态和控腿练习加以改善。

（四）仆步

1. 动作方法

一腿全蹲，全脚着地，脚尖稍向外展；另一腿自然伸直于体侧，脚尖内扣，全脚着地。如图 3-26 所示。

图 3-25

图 3-26

2. 技术要点

全蹲腿膝部与脚尖方向一致，另一腿平铺接近水平，伸出脚的脚尖与另一脚脚跟在一条直线上。

3. 错误纠正

初学者易出现全蹲腿脚尖没有外撇，伸出腿脚掌外翻等错误，如练习者身体柔韧性不好不能全蹲，可降低难度练习，并在平时多做压腿拉伸韧带的练习。

四、步法

基本步法可分为上步、退步、跟步、侧行步，等等。

（一）上步

1. 动作方法

后脚向前一步或前脚向前半步。如图 3-27、图 3-28 所示。

图 3-27

图 3-28

2. 技术要点

上体正直,身体重心稳定,上步时身体重量完全由一腿支撑后再提收另一脚向前,脚跟点地,然后过渡到全脚掌着地。

3. 错误纠正

初学者会出现身体重量没有完全由支撑腿支撑时就迈步向前,后脚主动用力蹬地,或不是前迈脚脚尖先着地后过渡到全脚掌着地等错误。平时练习注意强调太极拳行步练习时的点起点落、轻起轻落的特点。

(二)退步

1. 动作方法

前脚后退一步或连续退步。如图 3-29、图 3-30 所示。

图 3-29

图 3-30

2. 技术要点

身体中正,重心平稳。身体重量完全由一腿支撑后再提另一脚向后迈步,脚尖先着地,然后过渡到全脚掌着地。

3. 错误纠正

初学者会出现一腿支撑时重心不稳，前腿向后退步时蹬踏地面等错误。平时练习时多强调身体重心的转换过渡。

（三）跟步

1. 动作方法

后脚向前跟进半步。如图 3-31、图 3-32 所示。

图 3-31

图 3-32

2. 技术要点

身体中正，重心平稳，后脚上步时脚尖先落地。

3. 错误纠正

初学者也出现后脚蹬地用力上步的错误。平时练习要强调身体重心的转换和过渡。

（四）侧行步

1. 动作方法

两脚平行连续向一侧移动。如图 3-33、图 3-34 所示。

2. 技术要点

身体中正稳定，出脚脚尖先着地后重心再过渡到两脚之间。

3. 错误纠正

重心不稳，身体左歪右斜，出脚收脚没有做到点起点落。平时多做控体和重心转换练习。

图 3-33

图 3-34

第二节　太极拳运臂练习

太极拳的主要技法,如掤、捋、挤、按、采、挒、肘、靠等都要通过上肢动作来完成,太极拳有运劲如抽丝、连贯圆活、绵绵不绝、刚柔相济等特点。依靠上肢动作加以体现,所以有太极拳"根在腰腿、形于两手"的说法。进行运臂练习就是为了更好地针对太极拳练习中的各种手型、手法以及肩、肘、臂、腕、手指等上肢各部位动作要求而采取的练习。

一、分靠势

1. 准备姿势

身体自然站立,两脚分开平行与肩宽,两手垂于身体两侧。精神集中,呼吸自然,眼向前平视。

2. 动作方法

两臂徐徐向前平举高与肩平,距离与肩同宽,肩部放松肘微沉,沉腕舒指,掌心向前下方。如图 3-35 所示。

上体右转,两臂屈抱在胸前,两手上下相对成抱球状。右臂在上,右手高不过肩,左臂在下,左手低不过腰,两臂呈弧形,两手掌心相对。上体保持端正,眼看右腕。如图 3-36 所示。

上体转向前方,随之两臂交错向前上方和后下方分开。左掌停于体前,掌心向上,四指斜向前,高与肩平。右掌停于右胯旁,掌心向下,指尖向前。两臂分开后仍微屈呈半圆,眼看左手掌指。如图 3-37 所示。

上体左转,两臂在左胸前屈抱呈抱球状,左臂在上,右臂在下(如图 3-38 所示)。其他要求同右转。

上体再转向前方,随之两臂交错前后分开。右掌停于体前,左掌停于左胯旁,要求与左分靠势相同。左右反复练习。

图 3-35

图 3-36

图 3-37

图 3-38

3. 动作要领

（1）顶头沉肩，含胸竖脊，转腰运臂，协调一致。前臂向斜前方含有靠劲，后手向下有采劲，柔中有刚。抱球时两臂应该屈臂虚腋，圆满轻盈。

（2）刚开始练习时自然呼吸，动作熟练后做到分靠时呼气，抱球时吸气。

4. 提示口诀

左右抱球练分鬃，上靠下采似开弓。

转腰运臂劲完整，柔中有刚虚实分。

二、搂推势

1. 准备姿势

身体自然站立，两脚分开平行与肩宽，两手垂于身体两侧。精神集中，呼吸自然，眼向前平视。两臂缓缓前平举至两手与肩同高,松肩坠肘,沉腕舒指,掌心向前下方。如图3-39所示。

2. 动作方法

上体右转,左手经脸前向右划弧摆至右肩前,掌心向下;同时右手翻转下落,经腰侧向斜后方举起,高与肩平,掌心向上。眼看右手。如图3-40、图3-41所示。

上体转向前方,随之左手下落,经腹前向左搂至左胯旁,掌心向下,五指向前;同时右手屈收,经肩上耳旁向前推出,停于胸前,掌心向前,指尖与鼻尖平高,眼看前手。如图3-42、图3-43所示。

上体左转,右手随之经脸前向左上划弧摆至左肩前,掌心向下;同时左手翻转向侧后方上举,高与肩平,掌心向上,眼看左手。如图3-44、图3-45所示。

上体再转向前方,随之右手下落经腹前向右搂至右胯旁;左手屈收,经肩上耳旁向前推出,掌心向前,指尖向上,与鼻同高。眼看前后手如图3-46、图3-47所示。如此反复练习。

图3-39

图3-40

图3-41

图3-42

图3-43

图 3-44

图 3-45

图 3-46

图 3-47

3. 动作要领

（1）推掌时要沉肩、含胸、顶头、坐腕、舒指；搂时手经腹前向体侧划弧，运臂与转腰要协调，连贯圆活，一气呵成。

（2）刚练习时自然呼吸，动作熟练后做到搂推时呼气，转腰运臂时吸气。

4. 提示口诀

搂手推掌勤练习，转腰运臂要合一。

轻沉虚实巧变换，上攻下防显威力。

三、架推势

1. 准备姿势

身体自然站立，两脚分开平行与肩宽，两手垂于身体两侧。精神集中，呼吸自然，眼向前平视。两臂缓缓前平举至两手与肩同高,松肩坠肘,沉腕舒指,掌心向前下方。

2．动作方法

上体右转,两臂屈收,两掌在右胸前"抱球",与分靠势的抱球相同。如图3-48所示。

图 3-48

图 3-49

上体转向左前方,随之左手经胸前翻转上举,架于头部左上方,掌心斜向上。右手下落经胸前向左前方推出,掌心向前,指尖朝上,与鼻尖同高。眼看右手。如图3-49、图3-50所示。

两手下落,在左胸前"抱球",与分靠势左抱球相同。如图3-51所示。

上体转向右前方,随之右手经胸前翻转上举,架于头部右上方,掌心斜向上；左手下落经胸前向右前方推出。掌心向前,指尖朝上,高与鼻尖平。眼看左手。如此左右势反复练习。如图3-52、图3-53所示。

3．动作要领

（1）架推时结合腰脊的旋转,身体重心在两腿间随势移动。

（2）推掌时注意转腰、顺肩、含胸、坠肘、塌腕、舒指。

图 3-50

图 3-51

图 3-52

图 3-53

（3）动作熟练后结合呼吸练习，做到"抱球"时吸气，架推时呼气。

4. 提示口诀

运臂架推腰为轴，左旋右转求自由。

沉肩坠肘轻塌腕，蓄吸发呼显刚柔。

四、捋挤势

1. 准备姿势

身体自然站立，两脚分开平行与肩宽，两手垂于身体两侧。精神集中，呼吸自然，眼向前平视。两臂缓缓前平举至两手与肩同高，松肩坠肘，沉腕舒指，掌心向前下方。如图 3-54 所示。

2. 动作方法

上体右转，左手翻转伸至右前臂下方与右掌心相对，两掌右前左后，随上体左转屈臂后捋，收至腹前，眼看右前方。如图 3-55 所示。

图 3-54

图 3-55

上体右转,两臂翻转屈收上举,右掌横于胸前,掌心向内,左掌指附于右腕内侧,掌心转向前方。如图 3-56 所示。

两掌交搭,两臂撑展向右前方挤出,与胸同高,两臂撑圆。眼看右前臂。如图 3-57 所示。

图 3-56

图 3-57

上体转向左前方,左掌经右掌上面向左前方平抹划弧,掌心向下。同时右掌略收,停于左前臂下,两掌心斜相对。眼看左掌。如图 3-58 所示。

上体右转,两掌后捋至腹前。如图 3-59 所示。

上体左转,两臂旋转屈收上举,两掌交搭在胸前,随之向左前方挤出(如图 3-60 所示)。左掌横于胸前,右掌四指附于左腕内侧。两臂撑圆,两掌心相对(如图 3-61 所示)。眼看左前臂。如此反复交替练习。

图 3-58

图 3-59

图 3-60　　　　　　　　　　　　　　图 3-61

3．动作要领

捋挤动作应与腰脊旋转协调配合，身体重心在两腿间随势移动。保持顶头、竖脊、沉肩、含胸、撑臂等要领。

后捋时两掌前后交错，前挤时两掌前后交搭，换势时两掌平圆抹转。

动作熟练后结合呼吸，做到捋的时候吸气，挤的时候呼气，转换时调整呼吸。

4．提示口诀

旋腰运臂练捋挤，走化发放打根基。

捋在掌心巧引进，挤在前臂人难敌。

平圆抹掌势不断，捋吸挤呼气力宜。

五、云手势

1．准备姿势

身体自然站立，两脚分开平行与肩宽，两手垂于身体两侧。精神集中，呼吸自然，眼向前平视。两臂缓缓前平举至两手与肩同高，松肩坠肘，沉腕舒指，掌心向前下方。

2．动作方法

上体右转，右手随之右摆，掌心转向内，左手落于腹前，掌心向下。眼看右掌。如图 3-62 所示。

上体继续右转，右手经脸前、左手经腹前同时向右云转划弧，至身体右侧时两手心翻转，变成右手向外，左手向内，头随右手转动。如图 3-63 所示。

上体向左转，两手上下交换，随上体转动，同时向左云转划弧，眼看左手。如图 3-64 所示。

上体继续左转，两手继续左云，至身体左侧时，两手同时翻转，变成左手心向外，右手心向内。如图 3-65 所示。

图 3-62

图 3-63

图 3-64

图 3-65

上体向右转动,随之右手经脸前,左手经腹前同时向右云转划弧。如此反复练习。

3. 动作要领

(1) 云转时两臂保持半圆形,不可直臂或过于屈肘。

(2) 云转路线成相交的两个椭圆形,动作要连续不断,与转腰相配合。

(3) 云手练习时呼吸自然。

4. 提示口诀

两臂运转练云手,左右转腰眼随手。

周身完整势连贯,呼吸调整任自由。

第三节　太极拳行步练习

一、上步

1. 准备姿势

身体放松自然站立,脚跟靠拢,脚尖分开,两脚成八字形,两手叉腰自然背于身后。心平气和,精神集中,呼吸自然,眼睛向前平视。

2. 动作方法

上体左转,屈膝蹲坐,身体重心移到右腿上,左脚跟提起,头转看左前方,如图3-66所示。左脚向左前方上步,脚跟轻轻落地,脚尖翘起,左腿自然伸直,身体重心落在右腿上,上体姿势不变。眼平视左前方(如图3-67、图3-68所示)。左脚轻轻收回,脚尖点地,再向前上步轻落,如此反复练习3～5次。左脚收回踏实,身体重心移到左腿,上体右转,右脚提起,改为右上步练习。然后反复轮换练习。

图 3-66　　　　　图 3-67　　　　　图 3-68

3. 动作要领

(1) 向前上步和向后屈收时,脚要轻提轻放,点起点落,虚实分明,重心平稳。上体姿势与高度保持不变。

(2) 屈膝屈髋,缩胯敛臀,上体端正舒松,呼吸自然通畅。

(3) 根据本人的实际情况安排练习的次数和身体重心高低。

4. 注意

控制好身体重心,上步时身体不要后仰,落脚不要过远、过重,收脚时不要蹬地、拖地;上步距离不要太小,腿要伸直。

二、进步

1. 准备姿势

身体放松自然站立，脚跟靠拢，脚尖分开，两脚成八字形，两手叉腰。心平气和，精神集中，呼吸自然，眼睛向前平视。

2. 动作方法

屈膝蹲坐，身体重心移至右腿上，左腿提起向前上步；身体重心继续前移，左脚踏实，左腿屈膝前弓，右腿自然蹬直成左弓步（如图 3-69～图 3-71 所示）；左腿稍屈，重心后移，左脚尖翘起向外转动（如图 3-72 所示），随之上体向左转动，身体重心移至左腿，左腿屈弓，右脚提起收在左脚的踝关节处；右脚再向前上步，右腿屈膝前弓，左腿自然蹬直成右弓步（如图 3-73、图 3-74 所示）；重心后移，右脚尖翘起外转，左脚提起再向前上步，成左弓步。如此左右交替反复进行。

图 3-69

图 3-70

图 3-71

图 3-72

图 3-73

图 3-74

3. 动作要领

（1）上体松正，重心平稳，动作连贯轻柔，两腿虚实分明。

（2）弓步时前腿屈弓，脚尖方向朝前。后腿蹬伸时脚跟随之转动调整，直到腿自然蹬直，脚尖斜向前方，两脚踏实。

（3）初学时采用自然呼吸，随着动作熟练逐步做到每步两次呼吸，即上步时吸气，向前弓步时呼气；后坐转体时吸气，后脚收时呼气。

4. 注意

初学者不能心急，收脚时脚尖收在支撑脚内侧点地支撑以稳定重心；上步时控制好落点，不要匆忙；弓步时身体重心三七开分置于两腿，后脚踩实；转体与进步协调配合，收脚时转体屈髋，上步时转体展膝伸腿。

三、退步

1. 准备姿势

身体放松自然站立，脚跟靠拢，脚尖分开，两脚成八字形，两手叉腰。心平气和，精神集中，呼吸自然，眼睛向前平视。

2. 动作方法

屈膝蹲坐，身体重心移在右腿上，左脚轻轻提起后退一步，脚尖点地（如图3-75所示）；身体重心渐渐移到左腿，左脚踏实，右脚扭直，脚前掌着地成右虚步（如图3-76、图3-77所示）；右脚轻轻提起，后退一步，脚尖点地；身体重心后移，左脚扭直，脚前掌着地，成左虚步（如图3-78、图3-79所示）。如此反复交替进行退步的练习。

图 3-75

图 3-76

图 3-77

图 3-78

图 3-79

3. 动作要领

（1）身体中正，虚实分明，呼吸自然。

（2）虚步时，身体重心大部分落于后腿，前腿稍屈，脚尖朝前，后脚尖斜向前方。

（3）初学时用自然式呼吸，随动作熟练逐渐过渡为一步一呼吸，即提脚退步为吸，后坐虚步为呼。

4. 注意

落脚时两脚保持适当宽度，左右横向距离约为 20 厘米；要屈腿落胯，膝关节松活，下肢稳固，上肢放松；动作轻柔匀缓，控制好身体重心。

四、侧行步

1. 准备姿势

身体放松自然站立，脚跟脚尖靠拢，两手叉腰。心平气和，精神集中，呼吸自然，眼睛向前平视。

2. 动作方法

屈膝蹲坐，身体重心移到右腿，上体右转，左脚提起向左侧移动一步（如图 3-80 所示）；上体左转，身体重心左移，左脚踏实（如图 3-81 所示），右脚收拢并步，两脚平行朝前，相距 20 厘米（如图 3-82 所示）；上体右转，重心右移，左脚再向左侧移动一步；右脚收拢并步，动作同前。如此反复练习。

图 3-80

图 3-81

图 3-82

3. 动作要领

（1）头颈正直，沉肩含胸，上体中正，松腰活髋，重心平稳，脚步移动轻起轻落，动作连贯均匀。

（2）初学时自然呼吸，逐渐过渡到一步一呼吸。

4. 注意

动作完成过程中上体不要左歪右斜；分脚、并脚时重心完全放在支撑脚上；并步时两脚靠拢要有间距；注意活腰、转体。

五、跟步

1. 准备姿势

身体放松自然站立，脚跟靠拢，脚尖分开，两脚成八字形，两手叉腰。心平气和，精神集中，呼吸自然，眼睛向前平视。

2. 动作方法

屈膝蹲坐，左脚向前上步，重心前移，左腿屈弓成左弓步；右脚轻轻提起收拢半步，脚前掌落在左脚后面与前脚的距离约有本人的一脚长（如图 3-83 所示）；身体重心后移，右脚踏实，右腿屈坐，左脚提起向前移动小半步，脚跟着地，脚尖上翘，成左虚步；上体左转，左脚尖外撇，身体重心前移，右脚前进一步，右腿屈膝前弓成右弓步；左脚跟进半步落在右脚后面，身体重心后移，右脚向前移动小半步，脚跟着地成右虚步。如此左右轮换进行练习。

图 3-83

3. 动作要领

重心移动要平稳，上体始终保持松正，两脚提落要轻灵。

初学时自然呼吸，逐步做到弓步、虚步时呼气，转换时呼气。

4. 注意

收脚跟步要轻提轻落，控制好身体重心，重心转换过程要清楚。

第四节　太极拳推手练习

太极拳推手对练套路基本动作我们选择了定步推手基本技法练习，主要分单推手和双推手两部分。通过推手基本技法的练习，达到功力的培养和熟悉技法的运用。首先要掌握太极拳推手对练各种技法的规范要求，逐步领会和掌握推手过程中攻守进退、虚实刚柔、相互转化的基本规律;理解在粘黏连随的状态中立身中正、重心稳定、劲路柔韧、转换灵活、上下相随、整体协调的相互关系和基本原则,以及技法的运用。本书仅介绍基础入门的单推手练习。

一、立圆单推手

(1) 预备姿势及搭手。

甲乙相对站立,相对距离3米左右,身体自然放松,目视前方;行抱拳礼;重心略向右移,左脚轻轻抬起,脚尖外摆向前探出,身体自然下沉,成叉步,重心前压,同时两手从体侧向胸前交叉,右手在外,弧形向上分掌;右脚向前上步脚跟落地,脚尖翘起,同时左手叉腰,右手顺势向前弧形挥出,手指舒展,虎口圆撑;用小臂外侧与对方相搭于胸前,此为搭手定式。注意:两手相搭时,手心先向内后向外,五指斜向上,暗含螺旋力。(如图3-84~图3-86所示)

图 3-84

图 3-85

图 3-86

(2) 甲用右手指尖向乙面部伸插,重心略向前移,右腿随之前弓(如图3-87所示);乙以右手用掤劲承接甲之来劲,顺势重心略后移,左腿屈膝,向右转体,将甲右掌引向头部右前侧,使其落空。如图3-88所示。

(3) 乙顺势将右掌置甲右手腕上,向下绕弧切按,随即重心前移,右腿前弓,用右手指尖向前伸插甲腹部;甲以右手用掤劲承接乙来劲,右臂顺势回收,同时重心后移,屈左腿,向右转体,将乙右手引向体右胯侧,使其落空。如图3-89所示。

图 3-87

图 3-88

图 3-89

（4）甲再将右手弧形上提至头部右侧向乙面部伸插；乙仍如前顺势将甲右手引向头部右前侧，使其落空。如图 3-90～图 3-92 所示。

图 3-90

图 3-91

图 3-92

如此循环练习,双方推手路线成一立圆形,方向可互换,结束动作定止于搭手。如图 3-93、图 3-94 所示。

图 3-93

图 3-94

立圆单推手亦可出左足在前,搭左手练习。

要求:两人搭手推成立圆,劲力要顺势连贯,勿丢勿顶,同时动作注意沉肩垂肘,圆活自然。

二、腹前平圆(乾坤运转)

(1)预备姿势及搭手。如图 3-95～图 3-97 所示。

图 3-95

图 3-96

图 3-97

(2)由搭手向腹前下按,四指略向外轻搭于对方小臂;甲向对方腹前平按推出,乙重心回移并顺势松肘,使甲的按推之力落空于左腹前,并顺势转腰将其化于右腹。如图 3-98、图 3-99 所示。

图 3-98

图 3-99

(3) 乙重心前移,顺势向甲方腹前平按推出,甲方重心回移,顺势松肘,使乙的按推之力落空于左腹前,并顺势转腰将其化于右腹。如图 3-100、图 3-101 所示。

图 3-100

图 3-101

如此循环练习,双方推手路线在腹前成一平圆(如图 3-102～图 3-104 所示),结束动作止于搭手。如图 3-105、图 3-106 所示。

图 3-102

图 3-103

图 3-104

图 3-105

图 3-106

平圆单推手亦可出左足在前,搭左手练习,亦可反向。

要求:两人由搭手在腹前相合时,手掌以小指带动自然外展,与对方手臂相黏,手掌与地面相平;在保持立身中正的前提下,动作幅度尽可能大,重心进退明显,同时两手掌运行轨迹不可忽高忽低,需连贯自然,保持劲力的轻盈与流畅;目光及神意随手的变化而变。

三、太极运转(鱼摆尾)

(1)预备姿势及搭手。如图 3-107~图 3-109 所示。

图 3-107

图 3-108

图 3-109

(2)双方由搭手向内旋转手臂,肘关节随势而起,手臂自然保持弧形,双方手背轻贴于胸前(如图 3-110 所示);左手向左后方弧形上举并略向外撑,手心向外;双方自然呈太极图形;甲重心前移,手臂前掤,乙重心后移,身体略微左转,同时手臂回引于左侧胸前,同时手腕放松。如图 3-111 所示。

图 3-110

图 3-111

（3）乙顺势转腰，将甲的前掤之力化于身体右侧。如图 3-112 所示。

图 3-112

（4）乙重心前移，手臂前掤，甲重心后移，身体略微左转，同时手臂回引于左侧胸前，同时手腕放松。如图 3-113、图 3-114 所示。

图 3-113

图 3-114

如此循环练习，双方推手路线在胸前呈太极阴阳鱼，结束动作止于搭手。如图 3-115、图 3-116 所示。

图 3-115

图 3-116

太极运转亦可出左足在前,搭左手练习,亦可反向。

要求:双方手腕放松,在练习过程中手背手腕始终相贴,劲力有如鱼摆尾;在练习过程中,重心移动要始终保持平稳;后手向远方支撑与前手呼应,随势而动,不可随意松懈摇摆;劲力圆活,气势舒放,始终关注于双方身前身后的精神意识变化及手臂手腕运行劲力所形成的太极球。

四、折叠单推手

(1)预备姿势及搭手:与太极运转相同。如图 3-117~图 3-119 所示。

图 3-117

图 3-118

图 3-119

(2)甲右手向乙面部内旋伸插(掌心向下),重心向前移,右膝前弓;乙以右手用掤劲承接甲之来劲,重心稍后移,左腿屈膝,向右转体,将甲右手引向头部右侧;乙继续向右转体,坐胯,右臂外旋,掌心向上,掌背压于甲右手腕上,向下绕弧引带将甲右手沉压至右胯旁。如图 3-120、图 3-121 所示。

图 3-120

图 3-121

(3) 乙顺势将右手内旋循弧线上提，向甲面部伸插，重心随之前移，右腿前弓；甲右手黏随乙右手来势，重心后移，左腿屈膝，身体右转，将乙右手引向头部右侧；甲继续转腰坐胯，右臂外旋使掌心向上，掌背压乙右手腕上，向下绕弧引带将乙右手沉压至右胯旁。如图 3-122、图 3-123 所示。

图 3-122

图 3-123

(4) 甲顺势将右手内旋绕弧线上提向乙面部伸插；乙又以右手用掤劲承接甲之来劲，重心后移，转腰坐胯，将甲右手引向头部右侧（如图 3-124 所示），结束动作止于搭手。如图 3-125、图 3-126 所示。

图 3-124

图 3-125

图 3-126

如此循环练习，此练习亦可左足在前，搭左手进行。
要求：走化对方来势时，要注重转腰。

五、平圆单推手（胸前平圆）

(1) 预备姿势及搭手。如图 3-127～图 3-129 所示。

图 3-127

图 3-128

图 3-129

要求：双方搭手时，注意手腕与肩平，各含"掤劲"，既不可过于用力相顶抗，亦不可软而无力。

（2）甲身体重心略向前移，右腿前弓，以右掌向前平推，按向乙右胸部。如图 3-130 所示。

图 1-130

（3）乙承接甲之按劲，重心稍后移；左腿稍屈，上体右转，以右掌向右引甲右手，使其不能触及胸部而落空。如图 3-131 所示。

图 3-131

（4）乙随即顺势用右掌向前平推，按向甲右胸部。如图 3-132 所示。

图 3-132

（5）甲同样用右手承接乙之按劲，重心稍后移；左腿稍屈，上体右转，以右掌向右引乙右手使其落空。如图 3-133、图 3-134 所示。

图 3-133

图 3-134

动作止于搭手，如图 3-135、图 3-136 所示。

图 3-135

图 3-136

如此循环练习，双方推手路线成一平圆形。平圆单推手可左足在前换左手练习，方法相同。

要求：一方用按劲推按对方时，对方则用"化"劲化开，"化"时应注意转腰、坐胯，以腰带手，协调一致。双方手臂要保持掤劲，进退相随，不可僵硬，动作粘黏连随，不丢不顶。双方左手自然置于左侧。

第四章 九式太极操

本章内容主要介绍九式太极操,逐一将九式太极操的创编原则及要领、练习目标及重点、动作方法及要点做了细致的讲解和说明。九式太极操是以静为主、以动为辅的新型太极内功基础修炼方法,动作简单,易学易练,可于身形架势的开合动转和神意的静定与舒放之间呈现出太极健身所特有的整体和谐之美。九式太极操中的九个式子动作简朴,开合自如,舒展大方,动中寓静,静中寓动,宜静宜动,动转自然。作为一种新型太极健身项目,九式太极操拓展和丰富了社会化大众武术健身内容,将传统武术中的太极内功修炼和现代体操的练习形式相结合,既适用于群体和个人学练,也适合大范围推广和普及。

第一节 创编原则及要领

一、创编原则

九式太极操是以静为主、以动为辅的新型太极内功基础修炼方法,动作简单,易学易练,可于身形架势的开合动转和神意的静定与舒放之间呈现出太极健身所特有的整体和谐之美。其编创理念突出太极健身所带给人的舒展圆活、中正安舒的精神气质与神韵,以匀缓连贯、自然顺势如行云流水般的特有运动节律,促进人体周身气血的运行与畅达,提高身心的自我调节与修复能力,有效地减缓现代社会的精神压力,使练习者体会到太极健身的真实意蕴,回归松静自然之态,达到天人合一的境界。

在目前流行的现代武术健身方法中,最为常见的是武术套路练习。由于许多武术套路因其变化繁杂且难度较大,既不易于广泛推广,还易导致练习者过于执着于动作的表面形式,忽略对武术健身修心作用的深入理解。而被众多传统武术流派所推崇的内功养生修炼方法,如站桩等功法练习,在实际传播中,常常因为外形动作变化的单一和教学方法的保守,令初学者感觉枯燥乏味,从而失去了继续学练的兴趣,错失了运用传统武术健身的良好机会。

为了能在当前生活节奏日渐加快、生活压力日趋加重的社会环境下,更广泛地发挥传统武术内功修炼特有的健身养生和缓解身心压力作用,让更多人尽快感受到武术运动的乐趣与魅力,真实体验到练拳时身心的和谐一致、恬然忘我的境界,达到快速健身、调心和减缓压力的效果,通过对前人内修功法的提炼与变通,经过多年武术教学的实践与研究,在国家体育总局武术管理中心的直接指导下,总结创编了这套普及性强、适用面广的新型武术健身方法——九式太极操。

实践证明,九式太极操作为一种新型太极健身项目,拓展和丰富了社会化大众武术健身内容,将传统武术中的太极内功修炼和现代体操的练习形式相结合,既适用于群体和个人学练,也适合大范围推广和普及。对广大青少年太极健身的扫盲工作,为现代白领阶层提供效果显著的武术健身方法,都大有裨益,是缓解现代社会高压力人群亚健康状态的良好方式。

二、功法特点

九式太极操遵循太极健身原理,以畅通气血,体察虚实,舒展身心,活跃神意,培补元气为主要追求方向,既有普通体操动作简单、路线清晰、结构合理、易于群体学练的特点,又具有顺势自然、弧线运动、呼吸与动作相结合、匀缓连贯、劲力流畅和安神养元的传统太极内功修炼的主要特点。练习时动作自然连贯、绵绵不断、循环往复,强调内在的感受与体验,而不是外在形体的高难奇异。注重动作、神意与劲力的舒放,高度体现中正安舒、自然松静、内外和谐的精神状态,特别适合现代社会高压力生活状态下的人学练,符合全民健身所赋予的时代要求。

九式太极操中的九个式子动作简朴,开合自如,舒展大方,动中寓静,静中寓动,宜静宜动,动转自然。特别强调由动静变化所带来的神意收放、能量运转、内外虚实及重心之变换等要领,是一种使人直接进入空静圆活、动转自如、精神畅达的太极意境的有效途径和方法。

九式太极操多以双手胸前抱球为式与式之间的连接动作,可以根据练习者的个人喜好、身体状态、运动水平和练习环境,适当改变动作节奏与顺序变化,以增加练习效果和兴趣。例如,将定式时间适当延长则可成为传统拳术内功修炼的站桩练习,高水平的练习者还可以改变动作方向或顺势穿插一些自己喜爱的动作和变化。

九式太极操主体设计目标主要包括两个层面:静中求动,动中求静,通过修炼养生,体悟动静变化,缓解练习者身体与精神的紧张,以达到身心的和谐状态、精神舒畅,更加适合现代高压力生活状态的人群学练。

1. 以定式静力练习为主要目标的静中求动的太极筑基换力练习

静中求动的静是指形体不动、意念不乱,动是指元气的萌动。静中求动,就是以入静的手段达到元气充足的目的,是静到极静后的自然释放,其健身原理与功效近似传统武术内功训练中的站桩静练。

2. 以身形劲力变换练习为主要目标的动中求静的太极神意与身法练习

动中求静的动是指身形步法的动作的变换,静是指神态恬然、气息平和。动中求静,就是以松静缓慢的动作,达到神态恬然、气息平和的状态。在这种状态下,元气与心意、精神与形体协调统一,以内劲和神意的变化带动身形和步法的变换,其健身原理与功效类似传统武术内功导引训练。

三、主要功用

九式太极操是一种周身气血运行、意识与肢体高度配合的运动形式,通过意识与肢体的高度配合,内固精神,外示安逸,对身心的整体优化具有良好效果,通过缓慢的呼吸调理全身肌肉,有效地使呼吸深、长、细、匀,使练习者快速进入练习的最佳意境,对呼吸的平和稳定、肢体的协调控制和平衡感有较好效果。

九式太极操能在简约动作之中体现太极健身的整体运动法则,通过静练养生,再入动静变化,以至空灵妙用,动中得静,静中得定。其有助于练习者体悟太极健身中松静自然的精髓与奥妙,为进一步深入学习太极拳增加兴趣和信心,并可提高太极筑基换力、养元安神的功夫层次,使人体逐渐恢复到轻松安静、精神愉悦的身心状态。其动可以泻实,静可以补养,让练习者充分感受气血劲力的循环,加快进入太极健身的真实意境,使身体各部机能得到更为彻底的调整,尽快脱离紧张烦躁,逐渐恢复到轻松安静、精神愉悦的身心状态,更好地适应自然与社会环境的变化,是提高和恢复人体工作能力的有效措施之一。

依据"法于自然、阴阳平衡、动静相宜、身心合一"的太极运动规律,练习九式太极操可于动静、开合间逐渐加深加长呼吸,集中精神,将精神贯穿于呼吸与动作的和谐中,较快地调动、导引人体元气,疏通经络。通过动作开合和神意收放,充分调理呼吸,增大肺活量,使内劲浑厚饱满;通过左右动转、放松尾闾,充分调整全身,收提能量;通过太极圆弧动作,在开合、进退间令周身通畅;通过手臂的螺旋缠绕、松腰松胯和以腰带动身体肢节的运转,提高人体的协调性和灵活性,稳固下盘;通过松静自然与顺势利导,将身体的紧张与压力交于大地,有效地缓解肢体的紧张和疲倦,使人放松精神,回归自我。

九式太极操可充分达到太极健身在动作形式上的慢练效果,更好地体现太极拳健身原理,让练习者在简单的动作练习中体味太极健身静中寓动、动中寓静的美妙意境,体验神意回归后舒展的气势和通透的呼吸。唤醒人固有的自身修复潜能,使身体由僵紧变松活,使气运由憋闷到顺畅,调整到每个人的最佳状态,达到人体的动态平衡。

九式太极操以养生健体为根本目标,主张先修内再修外,注重太极修炼对人的心理情绪的调节和心境状态的调整,突出太极健身的真实意蕴与身心整体运动原则,强调松静自然、变化自如,既可自成体系按序练习,又可根据身体状态和功夫水平随意变化,使初习者也能较快地体验到太极的韵味与乐趣。

九式太极操亦可作为在从事各项紧张事务前心理减压和情绪调整的辅助手段,也可作为剧烈运动后的全身有氧调整练习。

四、习练要领

九式太极操除注重强身健体、祛病延年的保健功能外,还特别强调精神的拓展和心灵境界等内在功夫的提升。练习时应以身形中正安舒、动作柔和舒展、用意不用力、顺势连贯为指导方针,每一式都应注重身内感受与呼吸、神意的配合,目的是结合动作蓄运内气,舒筋活络,愉悦身心,调整状态。无论是定式练习或是动式练习,都应做到周身放松、不用僵力、心境平和、不急不躁,使身心处于自然祥和的状态中。只有动静和谐,很好地把握神意与真气的运用,才能真正体会周身各部位松与紧的变化感觉,根据动作意守全身相应部位,使身心内外得以调整和放松。

九式太极操特别强调呼吸与外形动作的紧密配合,在动式练习时保持身体不偏不倚、中正安舒,思想意念平静自由,不为身体外在动作所干扰。动中寓静,即以自身作为小宇宙,体察微妙的、平衡的"静";再由体内萌发的自然之动,催动肢体大开大合,即静中寓动。此"动"为静极而动的顺势而动,是均匀的、平衡的、精神高度放松的"动"。然后再求阴阳虚实之细微转化,内气自生,气运自如,达到身心的和谐状态。

练习时要特别注意胸部和心脏的放松,身体切忌紧张僵硬,上体保持正直,头正目平,下颌微收,虚领顶劲,两腋宜空、勿夹紧,肘部自然放松,两腿膝胯外撑,全身经络疏通。呼吸要求深、长、细、匀。握拳、开掌等动作的开合要随呼吸同步进行,并配合动作调息,意识贯注于丹田。同时以神意体察周身各部,使身形中正舒展,保持全身放松、舒适自然、挺拔伸展之姿。

九式太极操动作路线皆呈弧形,应注重以意领先以及稍节的运转,达到神意远放的意境。切忌用力过于强劲,性急则易致气滞而不通。同时,要把握此功法总体练习原则,即:松静自然,柔整连贯,顺势变化。松是指精神放松不紧张,意念放松不执着,肌体放松不僵滞;静是指心中平静不躁乱;柔是指动作柔缓,舒展飘逸,不用拙力;整是指心、意、气、身、手、足一动俱动,一静俱静;顺势变化是指要顺乎动作变化的内在规律。

其他部位要求做到竖项、齿扣、舌顶、垂肩、松膝、松腰。

竖项:下颌微向后收,不可用力,百会与会阴两穴的连线与地面垂直。

齿叩:牙齿轻叩,口唇轻闭,舌抵上腭,面部放松。

舌顶:舌尖自然抵住龈交穴内侧,增加津液,接通任督二脉。

垂肩:松肩,胸部放松,气沉丹田。

松膝:膝不可用力直挺,略有前屈之意。

松腰:随舌顶、肩垂、膝松及臀部略有下坐之意,腰部自然松弛下来。

第二节 练习目标及重点

一、练习者注意事项

练习九式太极操时,动作要走弧线并顺势而行,周身上下和谐一致,忌直来直去、动作僵紧。否则,得不到九式太极操特有的圆活趣味和顺势而变、动转自如的深层功夫。

九式太极操的奥妙是调整松静自然的身心状态,通过练习体悟周身上下阴阳虚实的运转变化,达到身体内外的高度平衡,要求练悟结合、身心并进。

要注意运动量的掌握,循序渐进,每次练习一定要留有余兴,勿急于求成,全套九式练习应以不少于连续三遍为宜。也可视个人的体力、兴趣和练功的时间长短,选练九式太极操其中一式或几式,练习数遍。

应注意对练习环境和周围气氛的选择,使身心愉悦,易于沉静。在每次练习时都要精神集中、心神合一、周身放松、自然合度。

着装宜宽松,尤其是裤子、鞋、袜以舒适为要,便于做下蹲、旋转等动作。

二、动作名称

第一式 无极式

第二式 开步下按式

第三式　抱球开合式
第四式　左右动转式
第五式　全身调理式
第六式　手捧莲花式
第七式　螺旋缠绕式
第八式　安神养元式
第九式　松心减负式

第三节　动作方法及要领

一、无极式

【预备势】并步直立

两脚并拢，重心落于全脚掌，脚趾微微扣地，空出足底涌泉穴；两臂自然下垂，手心向内；目光平视，全身放松。如图4-1所示。

【起势】开步直立

左脚脚跟、脚尖依次轻轻提起，向左横开半步，点起点落，由足尖至脚跟缓缓踩实，与肩同宽；重心随之移至两腿之间，两臂自然垂于体侧成开步直立。如图4-2所示。

1. 静立调息

保持开步直立姿势，在松静自然的基础上调整呼吸，逐渐使呼吸深、长、细、匀，胸背和身形自然舒展，头颈放松，精神舒畅。如图4-3所示。

图4-1

图4-2

图4-3

2. 握拳舒掌

松肩、松肘、松手,臂、指向下依次延展;双手缓缓做握拳、舒掌动作,将肩臂之力徐徐传递到双手;同时,下颌微收,头顶自然向上领起,身体呈松静挺拔之态。如图 4-4、图 4-5 所示。

如此重复做握拳、舒掌动作两次,要求手指充分舒展和回握自然。

3. 并步收势

左脚轻轻提起,收至右脚旁,两脚并拢,脚尖向前;身体自然直立,目视前方;精神内守,呼吸均匀平稳,保持放松入静状态。如图 4-6 所示。

图 4-4

图 4-5

图 4-6

【要领】

双手做握拳、舒掌动作时,呼吸要相应配合,自然调整呼吸,并将意念集中在颈肩、两臂与两手上。通过手部的动作和呼吸的调整,将肩背、胸部和腰部的紧张和压力逐渐放于脚下,足指自然扣地。同时,下颌微收,头向上顶,全身挺拔舒展、轻松舒适。

练习时要牙齿轻叩,口唇轻闭,舌尖轻抵上腭,要排除杂念,意存丹田,呼吸自然,气定神闲。在放松入静的基础上,神意远放,精神回收,要有"顶天立地、中正安舒、挺拔舒展"和"山崩于前而不惊,虎随于后而不恐"之神态与气势。

【功用】

无极式是学好、练好九式太极操的基础,依照拳术内功的基本要求,只有通过凝神聚气,由松入静,由静至定的过程,才能使身心沉静下来,不断感受和体悟练习时周身所产生的意气运行及劲力变化规律,达到中正安舒、神态端庄、意境虚无、松空挺拔、全身贯通、形神舒放和静极生动的良好状态,为练好后面各式做准备。

二、开步下按式

【预备势】并步直立

动作同无极式预备势,如图 4-7 所示。

【起势】开步直立

动作同无极式起势,如图 4-8 所示。

图 4-7

图 4-8

1. 旋腕按掌

双手略微后引外旋,拇指向上引领双手至与腰同高。手臂环腰际向前、向内回旋,按于胯侧;随之屈膝坐胯,双手轻轻下按,手指舒展,状似按球。如图 4-9、图 4-10 所示。

图 4-9

图 4-10

2. 沉身按掌

沉身下坐,敛臀松腰,双掌继续向下沉按,上身仍保持中正挺拔。

稍停片刻，松肩松腰，借双掌下按之势直立起身，两臂自然伸直并垂于体侧。如图4-11所示。

双手再次后引外旋，拇指向上挑领，环腰际向前、向内做弧形旋腕按掌和沉身按掌动作，至直立起身。

图4-11

图4-12

3. 并步收势

动作同无极式并步收势，如图4-12所示。

【要领】

做旋腕按掌动作时，要注意上半身的放松与挺拔，随着双腿自然下蹲，意和气要随之分别达于双掌掌心、手指和指尖。假想双手按在两个漂浮于水中的肥皂泡上，既不将肥皂泡按破，又不让肥皂泡离开水面。

做沉身按掌动作时，要求敛臀坐胯，尾闾放松，两腿顺势下蹲，膝不过足尖。意想将身体负担及压力渐渐移于两腿及脚下，使两脚涌泉穴与大地相接并有入地三尺的感觉；待身形稳定之后，意想将多余的身体负担及压力移至两手所按的假想的肥皂泡上，神意慢慢贯注于其上，并使其有托起全身之意。

【功用】

沉身下按式可使身体重心压于两腿与双足，自然达到身体上松下紧的状态，提高膝、踝关节的柔韧性和下肢的承受能力。久练可使尾闾、腰胯及膝部放松，下肢力量明显增强，达到松心降气、放松脏腑、稳固下盘之目的，全身自然生成蹬地拔起之势，增强手掌和身体对劲力变化的敏感度，培养练习者借势用劲的意识和能力。

三、抱球开合式

【预备势】并步直立

动作同无极式预备势，如图4-13所示。

【起势】开步直立

动作同无极式起势,如图 4-14 所示。

图 4-13

图 4-14

1. 屈膝抱球

两臂外旋,两手虎口张开,拇指向上,经由身体两侧向上挑领,至与肩同高时手臂自然远伸,手心向前,手指舒展。然后,沉肩坠肘,两掌向前、向内合抱至胸前,顺势沉身下蹲,成屈膝抱球状。如图 4-15、图 4-16 所示。

图 4-15

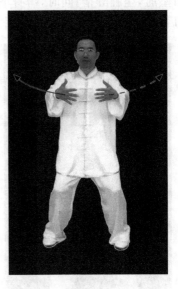

图 4-16

2. 抱球开合

开:两臂自然撑圆并向前弧形掤出,然后双手随势向身体两侧平展拉开至与肩平,肩肘略微下沉;同时,两腿向上蹬伸,身体直立挺拔。如图 4-17 所示。

图 4-17

图 4-18

合:沉肩坠肘,两臂自然向前、向内回抱于胸前;同时,身体下蹲,成屈膝抱球状,如图 4-18 所示。如此反复抱球开合两次,还原成屈膝抱球状。

3. 抱球收势

两腿向上蹬伸,直立起身;同时两掌和两臂缓缓内旋并向前上方掤举。上领至与肩同高时,沉肩坠肘,坐腕舒指;同时,蹲身下坐。两掌按至腰际,借按掌之势顺势起身,成开步直立状。然后,并步收势。如图 4-19～图 4-22 所示。

图 4-19

图 4-20

图 4-21

图 4-22

【要领】

做屈膝抱球动作时，要注意松肩、松臂、松肘、松胸，应将神意贯注于两手中间，其意如抱一薄薄之气球，若稍加用力便被挤破，不用力即飞走。身形要有支撑八面之意，意守丹田和两手的劳宫穴。在屈腿下蹲时，松腰敛臀，裹膝坐胯，膝不过足，周身中正。腿部的弯曲角度可根据练习者的具体情况来调整。

做抱球开合动作时，要用意不用力，两肩、两臂不可僵硬紧张。精神集中在所抱之球上，待双手逐渐发热有抱球感后，意想所抱之球逐渐膨胀，双手既不能挤也不能压，逐渐外扩，尽量使手臂撑开撑圆，保持动作均匀、舒缓连贯和自然顺势。两手用意念向两侧远拉至充分伸展后，沉身坐胯，两手自然顺势向胸前回抱，凝神聚气于丹田。

目光应随动作之势或凝神回视或极目远放，呼吸要自然配合，神意由内向外开阔、空透，要有前后左右皆有依靠和周身整体开合之感。

【功用】

抱球开合式可充分调理呼吸，增大肺活量，有效排除体内的浊气，使呼吸柔、细、深、匀，气自然收归于丹田，能让练习者较快领会松胸实腹和周身中正的感觉，体验神意的远放与回收，舒爽精神，放松身心。两手臂的外掤开展、里收内合与腿部的蹬伸、屈蹲动作协调配合，不但可使肩颈及双臂肌肉得到锻炼和放松，增强腰腿和膝部的弹性力量，长久练习还可端正身形，培养出开中寓合、合中寓开、周身浑圆一气的饱满内劲，逐渐形成意到、气到、力到、内外合一的浑厚气势。因此，抱球开合式既是一项良好的拳术身形架势基础练习，又是一项重要的太极内功基础练习。

四、左右动转式

【预备势】并步直立

动作同抱球开合式预备势，如图 4-23 所示。

【起势】开步直立→屈膝抱球

动作同抱球开合式屈膝抱球，如图 4-24～图 4-26 所示。

图 4-23

图 4-24

图 4-25

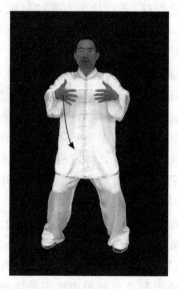

图 4-26

1. 右动转式

右手向下自然滑落至右侧小腹前，掌心劳宫穴向上，躯体右侧内脏和肌肉随之放松，将压力置于脚下。身体以脊柱为轴向右拧转，重心移至左脚；同时，右手顺势沿腰际转至身后，掌指内旋，虎口贴于命门，左手保持自然前掤。敛臀，坐胯，尾闾松开，沉身下蹲；同时，身体自然回转，右手手背经尾椎骨和臀部顺势向下滑落，并沿右腿外侧向身前弧形挑领至与胸平,虎口向上;两腿随势向上稍稍蹬起,略微起身,回复至屈膝抱球状。如图 4-27、图 4-28 所示。

图 4-27

图 4-28(a)

图 4-28(b)

2. 左动转式

动作与右动转式相同,唯左右方向相反。如图 4-29~图 4-32 所示。
如此左右交替练习两次,还原成屈膝抱球状。

3. 抱球收势

动作与抱球开合式抱球收势相同。如图 4-33~图 4-36 所示。

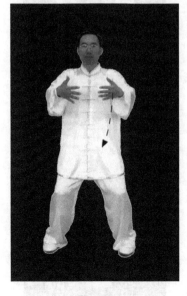
图 4-29

图 4-30

图 4-31（a）

图 4-31（b）

图 4-32

图 4-33

图 4-34

图 4-35

图 4-36

【要领】

当手臂向下自然滑落和手掌虎口向上领起时,身体两侧交替放松;先松同侧内脏,再松肩、松臂、松手,然后再调整腰部、胯部、膝部、踝关节。练习时,既要保持身体动转连贯、劲力顺畅,又要保持身形端正和腰背部的放松。随着两手的升降,神意应贯注于相应的左右两侧内脏和身体的放松,身体松到极松还要松,以身带手、以手领身、顺势自然引导肢体动作,使身形、劲力如行云流水般的顺畅,呼吸和神态保持自然。

【功用】

左右动转式通过交替放松身体两侧的内脏及肌肉,可达到舒肝健脾、劲力顺畅的效果,让练习者很好地体会身体内外的虚实变化,寻找到精神和形体放松的源头,做到从上至下依次自然地放松身体。内劲动转轻灵,神意收放自如,可使腰椎和尾椎得到自然的扭转和放松,有效避免和校正练习拳术时易于出现的凸臀和身体左偏右倚的现象。

五、全身调理式

【预备势】并步直立

动作同抱球开合式预备势,如图 4-37 所示。

【起势】开步直立→屈膝抱球

动作同抱球开合式起势,如图 4-38～图 4-40 所示。

全身调理式动作共由三个部分组成。

1. 伸展式

(1)沉肩,两腿慢慢向上蹬伸,直立起身,腰背略向后倚;同时,两臂顺势向前掤出,虎口撑圆;以手腕为轴,两手向下旋腕,翻掌至手心向前,掌指斜相对。双手向身体两侧划弧至与肩平。松肩沉身,屈膝下坐,两臂、两掌沿体侧顺势向下滑落至腰胯两侧,掌心向前。如图 4-41～图 4-43 所示。

图 4-37

图 4-38

（2）松腰、坐胯、沉身，双手顺势向身前旋腕翻掌至手心向上；两腿慢慢向上蹬伸、直立起身；同时，两手稍微回引，经身体两侧弧形上捧，至头顶上方时，两臂斜上举，手心斜相对。如图 4-44 所示。

图 4-39

图 4-40

（3）两手向脑后滑落，自然交叠于肩颈部，手背相贴；同时，下颌内收，两脚略内扣，腹部收紧，身体保持自然拉展状态。如图 4-45 所示。

图 4-41

图 4-42

图 4-43　　　　　　　　　　　图 4-44

（4）两手提拉上举，至头顶上方时，手臂自然伸展，略宽于肩，掌心向前；同时，头部稍向上仰，目光自然上视，腹部仍保持收紧，身体呈挺拔舒展状态。如图 4-46 所示。

【要领】

周身上下的动作都应以弧形相衔接，自然流畅，整体连贯。双手划弧时，五指自然舒展张开。要求以内带外，以外引内，神意随手部的运转而贯注于身体的相应部位，呼吸自然配合，劲力节节贯穿，身体呈挺拔舒展、浑圆饱满之势。

图 4-45（a）　　　　　图 4-45（b）　　　　　图 4-46

2. 捧水浇身式

（1）松肩沉身，屈腿下蹲，两臂经由体侧向下滑落至腰胯两侧。两手环抱，向胸前弧形领起。顺势旋腕翻掌，小指向上，手心向前，掌指斜相对。双手状似划水，向身体两侧划弧至与肩平。两掌弧形向下滑落至两膝外侧，顺势向上旋腕翻掌；同时，屈膝下蹲，沉身下坐，两脚稍向外开，膝肘相对。两腿慢慢向上蹬伸，身体直立，两手顺势于体前弧形向上捧至头顶上方，手臂斜上举，手心斜相对。如图 4-47～图 4-52 所示。

图 4-47

图 4-48

图 4-49

图 4-50

图 4-51　　　　　　　　　　　　　　图 4-52

（2）两手向脑后弧形滑落，指尖向下，中指和无名指轻触肩颈部。两肘顺势向两肋滑落，带动双手沿颈背向肩两侧拉开。松胸、松腰，屈膝下蹲，两臂向内相靠，指背相贴，拇指外翘，自然反合于胸前。双手小指侧轻贴胸口，沿身体中线向下滑落至小腹，然后自然分开，手心向上。两手环腰际向身后拉转，旋指、翻腕至掌心向外、拇指相对，其余手指自然交叠，两手背轻贴于两肾腧。松肩、松手，两手背轻贴于臀部向下滑落至两腿外侧；同时，蹲身下坐。直立起身，双臂借势反手经胸前弧形向上旋撑至与肩同高，臂掌撑圆，手心向前，手指相对。如图 4-53～图 4-59 所示。

图 4-53　　　　　　　　图 4-54　　　　　　　　图 4-55

图 4-56

图 4-57（a）

图 4-57（b）

【要领】

做捧水浇身式时，要想象两手先向上捧水，然后由上而下兜头一浇，身体疲劳随之被冲走。练习时应尽量保持动作的流畅连贯，全身顺势放松，身体的紧张和精神的压力经由动作的引领倾泻而出，交与大地，调整身心并使之逐渐进入到清爽松快的最佳状态。

图 4-58

图 4-59

3. 大伸展式

（1）双手向上、向两侧分掌划弧至与肩平；两腿屈膝下蹲、沉身；同时，两脚微微调整，稍向外开，膝与脚尖相对。两掌继续向下划弧，待划至胯旁时顺势向上翻掌，手心向上。直立起身，双手向体侧远伸并向头上捧起，两臂斜上举，手心斜相对，头部稍向上仰，目光自然上视。下颌内收，腹部微收，两脚内扣，两手向头后交叠于肩颈部，手背相贴，手指向下延伸，两肘上提，脊柱和身体充分拉展。如图 4-60～图 4-63 所示。

图 4-60

图 4-61

（2）两手向头顶上方提拉，然后自然旋臂成掌心向前，双臂略宽于肩并向上尽量延伸，全身充分挺拔舒展。下颌内收，腹部微收，两脚内扣，两手向头后交叠于颈肩部，手背相贴。双手中指和无名指轻触两肩，沿肩向两侧拉开，肘关节顺势沿体侧向下滑落，贴于两肋，成立腰开胸。松胸、松腰，屈膝下坐，两手向内相靠于胸前，小指侧轻贴胸口，指背相贴，拇指外翘，呈反合十字状。如图 4-64～图 4-67 所示。

图 4-62

图 4-63

图 4-64

图 4-65

图 4-66

图 4-67

（3）沉身，两手向下滑落至腹前时向外分开。两腿慢慢向上蹬伸，直立起身，两手顺势向身体两侧弧形拉展，掌心向前，拇指向上挑领至与肩平。如图 4-68、图 4-69 所示。

（4）屈膝沉身，双手顺势向胸前合抱，还原至屈膝抱球。如图 4-70 所示。

（5）抱球收势，动作与抱球开合式抱球收势相同。如图 4-71～图 4-74 所示。

【要领】

做大伸展式时，神意应随动作的开合而收放。双手上举时，两臂尽量向上拉伸，运用上提、下坠之势使周身关节充分舒展拔长。在呼吸舒适的前提下，全身始终保持自然舒展和浑厚挺拔，有如猫伸懒腰之伸展，动物晒毛之惬意。

图 4-68

图 4-69

图 4-70

图 4-71

图 4-72

图 4-73

图 4-74

【功用】

全身调理式可充分调理全身，使呼吸、神意和身体协调配合，通过呼吸和动作的调整将浊意、浊气、浊力释放于体外，使体内气血活跃、精神振作，亦可使脊椎拔长，肩颈放松，劲力达于梢节，全身挺拔舒展。通过松和紧、束和展的训练，获得拳术练习所要求的神意与劲力的和谐流畅，让身体得到较好的放松与拉展，消除长期伏案工作造成的紧张和压力，并对因错误姿势而导致的驼背有显著的矫正效果。

六、手捧莲花式

【预备势】并步直立

动作同抱球开合式,如图 4-75 所示。

图 4-75

【起势】开步直立→屈膝抱球

动作同抱球开合式屈膝抱球。如图 4-76～图 4-78 所示。

1. 前捧莲花(A)

沉肩,两腿向上蹬伸直立,小臂顺势向下,双手虎口撑圆,以手腕为轴,由下至上旋腕翻掌至小指向上、掌心朝前、掌指斜相对。双手向身体两侧自然划弧,至与肩平时双腿顺势下蹲。同时,沉肘松胯,双手自然向下滑落,经由腰部向身前弧形上捧与肩同高,小指侧相贴,掌心向上,五指张开呈手捧莲花状。(如图 4-79～图 4-81 所示)

图 4-76

图 4-77

图 4-78

图 4-79　　　　　　图 4-80　　　　　　图 4-81

2. 左捧莲花

双手向胸前回带，掌背自然相贴，靠近胸口膻中穴时沿身体中线向下、向前，再弧形向上反旋，反掌撑于胸前，掌心劳宫穴向外。身体左转 90°；右脚脚尖内扣，顺势向后撤步；两手动作保持不变。沉身坐胯，重心后移；左脚跟随之内旋，前脚掌内侧点地成左虚步；同时，以身带手，两臂外撑，两手向体侧弧形拉开至与肩同高。右脚向前蹬送，左脚顺势大步前迈，重心移至左腿，右脚随之跟进半步，脚掌内侧着地，脚尖自然外摆；同时，沉肘松胯，双手自然向下滑落，经由腰部向身前弧形上捧至与肩同高，小指侧相贴，掌心向上，掌指张开呈手捧莲花状。如图 4-82～图 4-87 所示。

图 4-82　　　　　　图 4-83　　　　　　图 4-84

图 4-85　　　　　　　　图 4-86　　　　　　　　图 4-87

3. 右捧莲花

两掌略向前伸，右脚后撤半步。身体后坐，重心随之后移；两手手背相贴，反向内旋并向胸前回收；左脚脚尖翘起。同时，左脚回收，脚尖点地成左虚步。两手内旋前伸，反掌撑于胸前；同时，左脚向前探出，脚尖翘起；身体重心不变。以身体为轴，左脚向内旋扣，身体右转90°；以身带手，两臂向外撑展。身体继续右转90°，重心移至左脚，成右虚步；同时，两手随身体的转动向身体两侧弧形拉开。右脚向前迈一大步，重心移至前腿，左脚随之跟进半步，脚掌内侧着地，脚尖自然外摆；双手顺势在身前划弧，合掌前捧至与肩同高，呈手捧莲花状。如图 4-88～图 4-94 所示。

图 4-88　　　　　　　　　　　　　图 4-89

图 4-90

图 4-91

4. 前捧莲花(B)

两掌略向前伸,左脚后撤。身体重心后移,右脚脚尖点地成右虚步,两手收回至胸前,手背相贴。右脚向前探出,脚尖翘起,重心落于左腿;两手内旋再向前反掌撑出。右脚内扣,身体左转,重心右移,两手向体侧撑展拉开。调整重心,左脚收至与肩同宽。同时,双腿屈蹲下坐;两手借势向下、向内、向上划圆向胸前弧形合掌上捧,呈手捧莲花状。如图 4-95～图 4-100 所示。

图 4-92

图 4-93

图 4-94　　　　　　　图 4-95　　　　　　　图 4-96

图 4-97　　　　　　　　　　　图 4-98

图 4-99　　　　　　　　　　　图 4-100

5. 屈膝抱球

双手内旋回收至胸口,指背相贴,沿身体顺势向下滑落至腹部。直立起身;两臂顺势向外分开,拇指向上,手心向前,经由身体两侧弧形向上挑至与肩平。

双腿屈蹲,沉身下坐,双手自然向胸前环抱成屈膝抱球。如图 4-101~图 4-103 所示。

图 4-101

图 4-102

图 4-103

6. 抱球收势

动作与抱球开合式抱球收势相同。如图 4-104~图 4-107 所示。

图 4-104

图 4-105

图 4-106

图 4-107

【要领】

做手捧莲花动作时，小臂、手指、手腕和肘关节的旋转要自然联动。双手向胸前远伸，两臂微屈，掌指舒展张开，腰腹收紧，腰背后倚，身形保持端正、对拔拉长。手臂动作应与身体的动转和步法的进退相呼应，步型稳定，并保持动作定式时前膝不超过脚尖。精神内守，凝神于掌指，目光自然远视或回收，神意贯注手指的转动和内脏的变化，脏腑放松，松胸顺气，全身上下和谐。

【功用】

手捧莲花式能使练习者很好地体会身形及动作的弧形转化，把神意收聚于身内，可使全身得到充分的休息，体现出九式太极操有一松必有一紧、有一开必有一合、有一收必有一放的特点，并可有效地练习手指、手腕、小臂和肘关节的自然联动，使身体进退自如，步法灵活，周身动作圆活顺畅。

七、螺旋缠绕式

【预备势】并步直立

动作同抱球开合式，如图 4-108 所示。

【起势】开步直立→屈膝抱球

动作同抱球开合式屈膝抱球，如图 4-109～图 4-111 所示。

（一）右螺旋缠绕式

1. 右螺旋缠绕反穿掌

身体右转 90°，重心左移；左手不动，右掌掌心向上，顺势向腹前回带；右脚脚尖点地成右虚步。沉身坐胯，右脚大步前探、脚尖翘起，右膝前挺；同时，右手经身体右侧反掌向身前划弧，左手顺势附于右肘内侧。左腿向前蹬送，身体重心前移，成右弓步；右手向前反穿至手臂伸直,与肩同高,掌心斜向上。如图 4-112～图 4-114 所示。

图 4-108

图 4-109

图 4-110

图 4-111

2. 旋臂坐身云掌

屈左膝,重心后移至左脚,沉身坐胯,右脚尖翘起,右手掌心向上、逆时针方向向额前旋臂划弧做云掌动作。如图 4-115 所示。

3. 右弓步片旋掌

左脚向前蹬送,重心前移成右弓步;同时,右手手心向上,以肘为轴继续向前划弧,旋至手臂伸直,左手仍附于右肘内侧。如图 4-116 所示。

图 4-112

图 4-113

图 4-114

图 4-115

图 4-116

4. 转身抹掌抱球

重心后移,身体后坐,然后扣右脚向左转身,以身带手,两掌交叉,左手在上、右手在下,向身体两侧平抹拉开,手心斜相对;重心移至右腿,身体继续左转,以手领身向身体两侧划弧至两臂环抱,顺势收左脚成左虚步抱球。如图 4-117、图 4-118 所示。

5. 左弓步挥臂旋按

左脚向前迈一步,重心前移成左弓步;同时,左臂向身前弧形挥出至与肩同高,掌心向上,右手顺势附于左肘内侧。重心后移至右腿,左脚矫健翘起;身体随之左转,以身带手,左臂向身体左侧弧形回领；同时沉身坐胯，左臂顺势做沉肘、旋掌、坐腕动作。重心前移，左手立掌向前弓步推出。如图 4-119～图 4-121 所示。

图 4-117

图 4-118

图 4-119

图 4-120

图 4-121

6．左右侧弓步掤手

（1）右掤：沉身坐胯，身体借势右转，重心右移成右侧弓步；同时，右脚脚尖翘起，以右脚跟为轴向外旋摆；以身带手、以手领身，右臂经由小腹向身体右侧弧形上掤至与肩平，左手虎口向上，拇指上挑，左掌外撑，掌心斜向外。如图 4-122 所示。

（2）左掤：左手向上旋臂经面部向右、向下划弧，经由小腹向左上回掤，挑领至与肩平，右臂不动，同时左脚内扣，身体重心左移，成左侧弓步。如图 4-123、图 4-124 所示。

图 4-122

图 4-123

图 4-124

7. 屈膝抱球

身体略向后倚，以两手梢节带动两臂向身后拉展；同时，借两臂向前回弹之力，双手向胸前合抱；借势将右腿轻轻收回半步，至两脚与肩同宽，成屈膝抱球。如图 4-125 所示。

图 4-125

8. 抱球收势

动作与抱球开合式抱球收势相同。

（二）左螺旋缠绕式

与右螺旋缠绕式动作相同，方向相反。如图 4-126～图 4-143 所示。

【要领】

所有动作应连贯自如，中间不能出现停滞和断续，注意体会及运用身体的沉身坐胯之势和以躯干动转带动手臂和腰腿拧转的借势用力。周身动作圆活自如，松静开展，呼吸及劲力保持顺畅自然。

【功用】

螺旋缠绕式为传统拳术身法、步法、手法和劲法的练习，充分体现了肢体的螺旋缠绕与身体的盘旋拧转，能使人周身协调、动转自如，并能使下盘灵活稳固，提高意、气、劲、形有序化配合的技能，培养"一扬手顾及四面，一动脚照料八方"的能力。

图 4-126

图 4-127

图 4-128

图 4-129

图 4-130

图 4-131

图 4-132

图 4-133

图 4-134

图 4-135

图 4-136

图 4-137

图 4-138

图 4-139

图 4-140

图 4-141

图 4-142

图 4-143

八、安神养元式

【预备势】并步直立

动作同抱球开合式预备势。如图 4-144 所示。

图 4-144

【起势】开步直立→屈膝抱球

动作同抱球开合式屈膝抱球。如图 4-145～图 4-147 所示。

1. 腹前合按

两掌向内向下旋按收至腹前,掌心向下,手指相对,凝神聚气,意存丹田。如图 4-148 所示。

图 4-145

图 4-146

图 4-147

图 4-148

2. 屈膝背手

腰背略向后倚,两手向前向外划弧,直立起身。两手继续环腰际向身后划弧至手背轻贴尾闾或命门处,手指自然交叠;同时,敛臀屈膝下坐。如图 4-149、图 4-150 所示。

  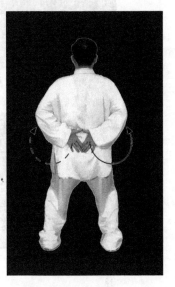

图 4-149　　　　　　　图 4-150(a)　　　　　　图 4-150(b)

3. 腹前回按

略微沉身,尾闾松开,身体向上直立,肩颈部和背部放松;两手向下自然滑落至体侧,并经身体两侧向上挑领至与肩平,手心向前,双手向内自然合抱。并借松腰坐胯之势,双手回按于腹前,松肩松手,沉身聚气,双脚脚趾自然抓地,神凝于丹田。如图 4-151、图 4-152 所示。

图 4-151　　　　　　　　　图 4-152

4. 收势

两掌向腹前和身体两侧弧形推按下压,借势蹬地起身成开步直立。左脚向右脚并拢还原至并步直立。如图 4-153、图 4-154 所示。

图 4-153　　　　　　　　图 4-154

【要领】

平心静气，神意回收，安神养元，两肩、两臂、两手放松，呼吸要保持深、长、细、匀，全身自然放松，意守丹田。

【功用】

练习安神养元式可促使丹田内气的运转，有助于腰部的放松和呼吸的深长。由于腰腹相连，丹田内气可随着呼吸的加深和人体的放松入静周转全身，帮助身体恢复元气，安神静心。

九、松心减负式

【预备式】并步直立

动作同抱球开合式预备势。如图 4-155 所示。

图 4-155　　　　　　　　图 4-156

【起势】开步直立→屈膝抱球

动作同抱球开合式屈膝抱球。如图 4-156～图 4-158 所示。

图 4-157

图 4-158

1. 掤臂按掌、直立起身

双手旋腕前掤至与肩平，沉肘坐腕、向胯旁沉身下按，直立起身。如图 4-159～图 4-161 所示。

图 4-159

图 4-160

图 4-161

2. 反手掸掌、松心减负

两手臂先向内旋至手背相贴，手指向下，手心向外，再提臂起肩，挺胸吸气，虎口及拇指沿身体中线由下向上提拉,至接近胸部时双手向外旋腕翻掌至手指向上,手背相贴。随后,两手迅速沿胸肋向下滑落掸手,似掸灰尘状,再向上拉展至与肩同高;内脏及全身肌肉彻底放松;同时,将气吐出,全身有如释重负之感。如图4-162~图4-164所示。

图 4-162

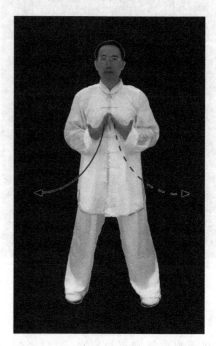

图 4-163

图 4-164

图 4-165

两臂向身体两侧拉开，顺势屈膝抱球。身体直立，两手内旋，两臂向前掤起至与肩平，沉肘坐腕，两臂顺势自然滑落于身体两侧，保持身体中正挺拔，神意放松，双手手背相贴再次由下向上提拉掸掌，沉身，两臂外开，顺势回收合按于腹前。如图 4-165～图 4-172 所示。

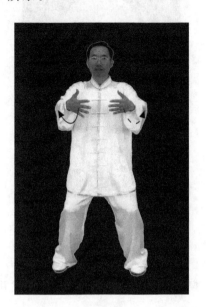

图 4-166

图 4-167

图 4-168

图 4-169

图 4-170

图 4-171

图 4-172

3. 收势

随身体直立，两掌贴身由内自外、由上至下，在小腹两侧画圆并垂于胯侧，还原成并步直立。如图 4-173、图 4-174 所示。

图 4-173

图 4-174

【要领】

充分吸气，充分呼气，内脏和肌肉完全放松，神意彻底舒展，完全将身体的紧张和压力交与大地。最后收势之时，应通过调整呼吸使身体达到松静自然的状态，保持神凝于内、身心静定。

【功用】

练习松心减负式可使肩部、颈部、胸部和全身肌肉放松,将身体多余的紧张和压力由上至下宣泄于大地,感觉全身轻松、心情愉快、精神舒爽并有如释重负之感。

附:

Form Ⅰ: *wuji* form

【Preparation】Feet Together, Standing Tall.

With toes touching and feet together relaxed and extended, let your center sink to cover the soles of the feet. The toes should gently press downward, and only the area of the Bubbling Spring point (*yongquan* acupoint) should not touch the ground. The arms are naturally suspended; the palms of the hands face inward; the gaze is level, and the whole body is relaxed. (Fig 4-1)

【Beginning Gathering energy】Stepping Out, Standing Straight.

Lightly raise the heel of the left foot, then the toes. Step sideways to the left about a shoulder's width, raising and lowering the foot slowly and deliberately. The center follows this movement, shifting to between the two feet, completing the movement. (Fig 4-2)

【Movement】

1. Calmly Standing, Shifting the Breath

As part of the movement "Stepping Out, Standing Tall" one is calm, maintaining a naturally relaxed foundation as one gradually shifts to a full breath by causing the breath to deepen, lengthen, and to become fine and even. The neck and back naturally relax and lengthen the top of the head relaxes, and the spirit is at ease. (Fig 4-3)

2. Making Fists, Relaxing Palms

In turn relax the shoulders, relax the elbows, and relax the hands. Gradually open and extend the relaxation downward from the upper arms to the fingers. With both hands gradually and lightly make fists while keeping the palms relaxed. The strength of the arms passes through the arms and transfers to the hands. At the same time loosen the jaw a little. Raise the neck and the top of the head rises with it, causing the body to appear relaxed and extended. (Fig 4-4, Fig 4-5)

Repeat the "Making Fist, Relaxing Palms" movement two times, completely and smoothly extending the fingers and then naturally and lightly forming fists.

3. Feet Together, Gathering Energy

Lightly raise the left foot and move it next to the right foot. Both feet are relaxed and extended, toes pointing forward, body naturally standing straight with the gaze forward. The spirit is concentrated within, the breath is even, and one maintains an attitude and appearance of calm. (Fig 4-6)

【Notes】
When both hands move in the "Making Fists, Relaxing Palms" sequence, the breath needs to accompany the movements of the hands, naturally and completely shifting the breath each time the hands clench and relax. One's intention is to unify the movements of the neck, shoulders, arms and hands in coordination with the shifting of the breath. From shoulders to fingers, from head to waist, let tension and stress gradually move toward the feet. At the same time, with the head feeling pulled from the top, slightly incline the neck. The whole body will then be stretched out and lengthened, lightly and naturally relaxed.

During practice, the mouth should be lightly closed, the teeth lightly touching together, and with the tip of the tongue lightly resting on the upper palate. One eliminates all personal preoccupations, placing the mind in the *dan tian*. The breath is natural, the *qi* is settled, and the spirit is idle. In this fundamental state of calm and relaxation, one's mind is detached and one's spirit is recollected. One aspires to having "the top of the head touching heaven while standing on earth." One will be centered, upright, peaceful and comfortable, extended, and happy. One will seek the posture and forceful stance of "with a landslide in front, not frightened; with a tiger following behind, not afraid".

【Significance】
The *wuji* stance is the foundation of the Nine-Form *taiji* Exercise. It should be practiced and studied thoroughly. The fundamental requirement of taiji quan inner work is a practice time focused on concentrating attention and gathering *qi*. Through relaxation one enters calm; through calmness one becomes steady. Once you first steady the body and heart, then you will be able to have a deep impression and realization through the body of changes in the body: its production of temperament and strength which become habitual. When you have become centered, upright, and peaceful; when your spirit is steady, the feelings empty, and you are relaxed, empty and extended, then your whole body opens up. Then the spirit is at ease yet alert in an ultimate calm, and the body, mind, and heart are united. With this foundation you will be well prepared to practice each of the forms which follow.

Form II : Stepping Out and Pressing Down

【Preparation】Feet Together, Standing Tall. (Fig 4-7)

【Gathering energy】Stepping Out, Standing Tall. Take *wuji* form. (Fig 4-8)

【Movement】

1. Rotating the Wrist, Pressing with Palms

Both hands drop slightly to the back rotating outward, thumbs pointing up leading the hands to waist height. Hands and arms circle to the front at waist height, returning to circle, inward, curving and pressing toward the *kua* area on each side. At the same time bend the knees and sit the hips, both hands lightly pressing down. The fingers should be relaxed and extended, and appear to be pressing a ball. (Fig 4-9, Fig 4-10)

2. Sinking the Body, Pressing with Palms

Sink the body into a semi-squat position. Draw back the arms and relax the waist. At the same time, the hands continue to press downwards, the upper body remaining upright and extended. Stop a moment, relaxing the shoulders and waist. Use the force of the palms pressing down to straighten and raise the body, naturally straightening and extending the arms at the sides. Both arms once more gradually circle outward and then forward along the waist, thumbs energetically pointing up. Then making an arc, return to the movement "rotating the wrist", and "sinking the body pressing with palms". Return to "standing straight and raising the body". (Fig 4-11)

3. Feet Together, Gathering Energy

This repeats the *wuji* form "Gathering Energy"(Fig 4-12)

【Notes】

When executing "Rotating the Wrists, Pressing with Palms", be sure that the upper body remains relaxed and extended. The body should naturally move into a semi-squat; the intention and *qi* should flow through the palms to the fingertips. The hands should feel as if they were floating on a soap bubble lightly so as not to break it, yet still preventing it from floating up from the surface.

When doing "Sinking the Body, Pressing with Palms", be sure to draw back the arms and sit the hips, relaxing the coccyx. The legs follow the energy, squatting down. The knees do not go past the toes. Imagine the other part of the body with force gradually moving down through the legs to below the feet. The ground and the feet are in relationship, connecting through each foot's Bubbling Spring points (*yong quan acupoint*) "as though to a depth of three feet". The spirit, mind and intention slowly flow to the hands which appear to be pressing a soap bubble. Imagine that one part of the body experiences pressure moving upwards as though to support the rising of the entire body.

【Significance】

"Sinking the Body and Pressing Down" causes the body's center to press through the legs and feet, naturally bringing about a state where the upper body relaxes and is drained of tension of legs. This increases the ability of the knees and the ankle joints to bear pressure. After long practice the lower spine, waist & hips and even knees relax. This increases the strength of the lower limbs, cultivates a relaxed mind and calmed *qi*, relaxes the inner organs, and attains the goal of a steady lower body. The movement naturally brings the entire body to a feeling of "crouching down before leaping upward". It enhances the strength and agility of the hands and body and nurtures the student's understanding and ability to use his energy and strength.

The Ⅲ Form: Holding the Ball, Opening and Closing

【Preparation】Feet together, standing tall. (Fig 4-13)

【Gathering energy】Stepping out, standing tall. Take *Wuji* form. (Fig 4-14)

【Movement】

1. Bending the Knees, Holding the Ball

Rotate the arms outward, with the *hukou* open, thumbs pointing up, and extend the arms lightly to the sides of the body. As the body rises and becomes upright, the hands are energetically drawn upward with the body to shoulder height, and are naturally widely extended. The palms face forward, the fingers are also relaxed and extended. Sink the shoulders and drop the elbows, the palms embrace the area in front of the chest. Following the energy, sink the body squatting down, taking the "Bending the Knees, Holding the Ball" position. (Fig 4-15, Fig 4-16)

2. Holding the Ball, Opening and Closing

Opening: the arms naturally maintain a circle, moving forward and outward, the hands following the energy outwards from the sides of the body, extending and pulling open to the level of the shoulders. The shoulders and elbows sink downwards somewhat, and at the same time the legs rise upward though remaining partly bent, causing the body to stand straight and extended. (Fig 4-17)

Closing: Sink the shoulders, drop the elbows, the arms naturally moving forward. At the same time the body squats, taking the "Bending the Knees Holding the Ball" position. (Fig 4-18)

In this way return to the "Holding the Ball, Opening and Closing" position two times, returning to the starting point "Bending the Knees, Holding the Ball."

3. Holding the Ball, Gathering Energy

Straighten the body and begin to rise. At the same time the hand, fingers and forearms rotate slightly inward, upward, and forward, until the palms facing out. When the hands reach shoulder height, the shoulders sink and the elbows drop, sit the wrists and relax the fingers. Sit the hips, and press the palms downwards toward the waistline. Use the energy of the downward-pressing palms to enhance the energy of the body as it rises, completing "Stepping Out, Standing Tall." (Fig 4-19～Fig 4-22). Then move to "Feet Together, Gathering Energy."

【Notes】

When executing "Bending the Knees, Holding the Ball", be sure to relax the shoulders, arms, elbows and chest. Place the attention closely on the space between the two hands, the idea being to hold a ball of air, lightly so as not to break it, but with enough strength to insure it doesn't fly off. The body should be so situated that if approached from any direction it would remain stable.

Attention should be fixed on the *dantian* and the *laogong* points. When bending the knees and squatting down, relax the waist and keep the arms back. Tuck in the knees and sit back on the hips with the knees not protruding over the feet. Keep the entire body centered. The angle of the legs adjusts according to the student's body type.

When executing "Embrace the Ball, Opening and Closing", one should use intention, not strength. Shoulders and arms should not be rigid or tense. The mind is focused inside the ball. After a while hands extend and become warm. In the imagination, the ball gradually expands outward without squeezing or pressing. The arms do not exert any force while gradually moving outward. The hands and arms smoothly open to form a circle. Peacefully follow the energy, carrying the arms open from the shoulders to the sides. Again using the imagination, pull the arms out from the sides far out to an extended fullness. Sink the body and the hips, the hands naturally following the energy, returning to hold the ball in front of the chest, turning the mind and *qi* to the *dantian*.

The gaze should follow the energy of the movement. Concentrate attention on turning the gaze far off into an infinite distance. The breath naturally accompanies the movement. The spirit goes from within towards the outer vastness to penetrate emptiness. In all this, from in front and behind, from right and left, one must rely on having the whole body upright, and a feeling of the whole body opening and closing.

【Significance】

The form "Holding the Ball, Opening and Closing" can improve the breathing, increase vital capacity, and is effective in eliminating bad *qi* from the body. It helps the breath become soft, fine, deep and even and helps the *qi* naturally accumulate in the *dan tian*. This leads the practitioner fairly quickly to a feeling of relaxation in the chest and rootedness in the abdomen, with the body centered and straight. He experiences the mind's moving outwards and gathering in, and achieves relaxation of mind, heart, and body. The alternating movement of the hands and arms, opening wide and extended, then gathering inward and returning, coordinating with the alternating movement of the legs, straightening and bending——this not only toughens and relaxes the area of the shoulders and neck to the muscles of the arms and legs, it increases reserves of strength in the waist and knees and legs. The practitioner maintain an erect posture, demonstrating "When the center is open, the dwelling closed/suitable; when the center is closed, the dwelling open." In the body is a natural circuit of one complete inner movement of the *qi*. Gradually, within the body, the mind, *qi*, and strength come together and the inner and outer and become one. This is the substantial, simple force of the one *qi*. Because of this inner movement of *qi*, "Holding the Ball, Opening and Closing" is a fine example of the boxing art's basic physical exercise; it is also an important basic training exercise for *Taiji* inner work.

The IV Form: Left and Right Turning

【Preparation】Feet Together, Standing Straight. (Fig 4-23)
【Gathering Force】Stepping Out, Standing Straight.
【Take the position of】Holding the Ball, Opening and Closing. (Fig 4-24~Fig 4-26)
【Movement】

1. Turning to The Right

The right hand naturally slips downward to the right side by the lower abdomen, with the *laogong* acupoint (in the center of the palm) facing upward. The inner organs on the right side of the body relax in a flow to the right foot. The lower spine functions as an axis, twisting to the right. Shift the center to the left foot, at the same time the right hand follows the energy along the waist, moving to the back of the body.

The palm and fingers rotate inward, the *hukou* touches the *mingmen*, the left hand naturally stays in front. With the arm back, sit the hip joints *kua*, keep the tail bone area open, sink the hips into a semi-squat. At the same time the body naturally returns to face front, the back of the right hand rests lightly on the tail bone (coccyx). As the body turns, the arm, slipping slightly downwards, follow the force along the sides to the right knee. The *hukou* faces up, moving to the front of the body in an arc to about chest height. At the same time the legs follow the energy, very slightly raising the body from the squatting position, then returning to bending the knees and the posture of " Holding the Ball ". (Fig 4-27, Fig 4-28)

2. Left Turning Movement

The left turning movement is the same as the right turning movement but in the opposite direction. Practice the combined movements of up, left and right turning two times, alternating sides, finally returning to the original "Bending the Knees, Holding the Ball." (Fig 4-29~Fig 4-32)

3. Holding the Ball, Gathering Energy

The same as the sequence, "Holding the Ball, Opening and Closing", "Holding the Ball, Gathering Energy."(Fig 4-33~Fig 4-36)

【Notes】

When the hands and arms naturally slip downwards, and the palms and *hu kou* rise upward, the two sides of the body alternately relax; first relax the organs on one side, then relax shoulders, arms, hands. Then again shift the waist, *kua*, and ankle. When practicing strength must flow smoothly throughout the body's turning movement; moreover the torso is carried upright with the waist and back relaxed, following the raising and lowering of the hands. The attention should be focused on right and left inner organs on both sides and on the relaxation of the body. One should strive for the utmost relaxation, relaxing further and further. Use the body to move the hands; use the hands to lead the body, allowing the energy to naturally guide the movements of the limbs and toss to. This causes the toss to move with strength as smoothly as clouds and as a boat through flowing waters. It results in natural breathing and posture.

【Significance】

"Left and right turning movement" moves and relaxes in turn the body's inner organs and muscles on both sides. The liver relaxes and the spleen elongates, and they become stronger and smoother. The student learns to distinguish between real and imaginary changes in the body, both internal and external. Seeking the spirit and form of the relaxed original mind; naturally working from upper to lower, naturally and successively relaxing the sides of the body——this develops inner strength and agility in turning. Spirit and Mind smoothly unite. The waist, lower vertebrae and tail bones move in a natural and relaxed twisting movement.

The whole form helps the students of boxing arts effectively avoid or correct the tendency of the buttocks to protrude or the body to lean to the right or the left.

The Ⅴ Form: Whole Body Adjustment

【Preparation】Stepping out, Standing Straight

Same as Holding the Ball, Opening and Closing. (Fig 4-37)

【Gathering energy】

Stepping out, Standing Straight to Bending the Knees, Holding the Ball. (Fig 4-38~Fig 4-40)

【Movement】

1. Body Extension

(1) Extending Wide, Sink the shoulders as the legs slowly raise the body from a squat. The torso, remaining erect, rises at the same time, and the waist and back lean slightly backwards. The forearms follow the energy as they move forward and out, the *hukou* circle around using the hands and wrists as an axis. The hands move upwards rotating the wrists, turning the palms until the palms face outwards, the palms and fingers of each hand in opposition. The hands move in an arc, up from the sides of the body until they reach shoulder level. Relax the shoulders, sink the body, bend the knees and sit the hips. The arms and hands slip down along the sides of the body, following the energy, past the waist, then the hip, with the palms facing forwards. (Fig 4-41~Fig 4-43)

(2) Relax the waist, sit the hip joints, sink the body, the hands following the energy toward the front of the body, rotating the wrists and turning the palms over so that the palms face upwards. The legs slowly extend upwards raising the body and keeping the torso erect. At the same time the hands rise upward in line with the sides, in an arc above the head, lifted in a full extension. (Fig 4-44)

(3) The hands move to the back of the head, slipping down naturally to the neck and shoulder area, the fingers touching the neck. At the same time bend the neck to draw energy inwards. The feet lightly grasp the ground, the stomach area becomes firm and taut, causing the body to pull into an extended position. (Fig 4-45)

(4) As the hands are carried upwards over the head, the hands and arms briefly and naturally extend to shoulder width, with the palms facing forwards. At the same time the head slightly tilts upwards, the gaze naturally follows. The stomach area is naturally taut and the body appears lengthened and extended. (Fig 4-46)

【Notes】

In this movement, the upper and lower parts of the body join in an arc, naturally flowing, smooth and connected. As they move, the hands and fingers are naturally relaxed and extended but not above the head. Let the inner carry the outer, using the outer to lead the inner, mind and spirit following the movement of the hands' turning and extending, paying close attention to the body's corresponding position. The breathing naturally coordinates with the movement, increasing the strength of the joints. The body appears naturally extended, encircling and fully containing the energy.

2. Carrying Water in Both Hands, Sprinkling the Body

(1) Relax the shoulders and sink the body, bend the knees and semi-squat, the arms lightly extending to the sides and slipping down to the waist and sides by the hip joints. The hands rise upwards in an arc, then in an encircling motion, face the chest. Following the energy, rotate the wrists and turn the palms over so that the little finger is up and the palm of faces forward. Palms and fingers of each hand are opposed. The hands seem to be parting water as they move toward the sides of the body, moving in an arc up to shoulder level. The palms arc downwards towards the outside of the knees. Following the energy rotate the wrists and turn the palms up. At the same time bend the knees and squat, sink the body and sit the hip. Slightly turn out the feet so that knees and feet of each leg point in opposite directions. The legs slowly straighten and extend upward. The hands move in front of the body to angle, arcing forward, as though both hands are carrying something up above the head. Then the hands and arms slant upward, and palms face each other. (Fig 4-47~Fig 4-52)

(2) The hands arc behind the head with the fingertips pointing down, the middle finger and ring finger lightly touching the nape of the neck. The elbow joints are closed. The hands then follow the energy from the back of the neck, pulling outward to the shoulders. Relax the chest, relax the waist, bend the knees and squat. The hands turn inwards and lean against each other, with the backs of the fingers touching, the thumb turned out, as the hands naturally return to a position in front of the chest. The little fingers lightly press the bottom of the sternum, following the center line of the body slipping down to the lower abdomen, the hands then naturally separating and opening. The hands are palm-upwards, then they circle the waist towards the back of the body. Rotate the fingers and turn the wrists over so that the palms face out, the thumbs opposing, the other fingers naturally following, so that the backs of the hands lightly touch where the kidneys. Relax the shoulders, relax the hands, the backs of the hand lightly press the

buttocks, then moving forward and slipping down towards the sides of the legs. At the same time the body moves to a semi squat. Raise the body and stand straight as the arms gather the energy, arcing upward, bringing the hands towards the front of the chest to shoulder height. The arms form a circle with the palms facing forward, fingers opposed. (Fig 4-53～Fig 4-59)

【Notes】

When doing "Carry water, Sprinkle the Body", one should imagine the hands as first rising together carrying water, then from the height sprinkle the head and rinse the weary body. The practitioner should fully embody a smoothly flowing continuous movement, the whole body relaxed and following the energy. The tension in the body and pressure on the spirit are led to pour out in torrents and leave, being dispersed into the earth. The body, erect and centered, gradually assumes a clear, relaxed, and beautiful appearance.

3. Great Extension

(1) The hands move upward. As the hands separate, moving in an arc towards the sides to shoulder height, the legs bend at the knees to a squat, sink the body; at the same time the feet slightly shift a little opening outwards, keeping the knee and toes aligned (opposite). The palms continue to circle downwards until, reaching the hip joints hip area, they follow the energy, reverse and turn palms up. Stand straight and raise the body, the hands extended fully, stretching up from the sides of the body to reach above the head, slanting the arms up, the palms slanting and facing each other (opposite), the head tilted a little up, the gaze naturally following. Lower the neck, gathering energy, the stomach area slightly tucked, the feet gripping inwards. At the same time the hands move toward the back and towards the area of the nape of the neck. The backs of the hands touch, the fingers are extended pointing down, the elbows raised, causing the spine and body to be pulled to its full extension. (Fig 4-60～Fig 4-63)

(2) The hands rise above the head, naturally rotating the arms bringing the palms to face forward. The arms are held slightly wider than shoulders and extend fully upward, causing the whole body to be fully and naturally extended. Bend the neck down to gather energy, the stomach area slightly tucked, the feet gripping inwards. The hands move behind the head toward the neck area. At the same time, the feet grip inward, the backs of the hands touch. The middle finger and the finger lightly move along, pulling open to the sides of the shoulders. The elbow joints following the energy along the sides of the body downwards pressing the ribs, completing "Erect waist open chest". Relax the chest, relax the waist, bend the knees and sit the hips, the hands and arms moving inwards leaning on the front of the chest, the little finger lightly touching the base of the sternum, the backs of the fingers of each hand touching each other, the thumbs turned out, so that the ten fingers are in a reversed position. (Fig 4-64～Fig 4-67)

(3) Bend the knees and sink the body, the hands moving downward in front of the abdomen and then opening outward. The legs slowly raise and extend. Stand straight and raise the body, the hands following the energy towards the sides of the body, extending in an arc, the palms facing forwards, the thumb energetically lifts upwards carrying the movement to shoulder height. (Fig 4-68, Fig 4-69)

(4) Bend the knees and sink the body, the hands follow the energy towards the front of the chest closing the embrace, returning again to "Bending the knees, holding the ball". (Fig 4-70)

(5) "Holding the ball, gathering the energy". The same as "Holding the Ball, Opening and Closing" and "Gathering Energy" form. (Fig 4-71～Fig 4-74)

【Notes】

When executing the "Great Extension" form, mind and spirit should follow the gestures of opening and closing, gathering and placing. When the hands are raised, the arms are fully stretched and extended. The movement uses rising and falling energy to fully relax, extend and adjust the body's stiffness and arthritic tendencies. The breath rises and falls accordingly. Throughout this movement, whole body should naturally relax, extend and expand. It will appear to move like a cat when it stretches, contented, basking in the sun that shines on its gleaming fur.

【Significance】

This form can fully readjust the inner body, assisting in coordination of breath, mind, imagination and body. In this coordination of mind and body, contaminated thoughts, qi, and energy are all set free and released from the body, causing the inner body's qi and blood to leap forward and the spirit to be invigorated. It also causes the elongation of the lower spine, the relaxation of the nape of the neck, and the lessening of constriction in the joints. The body becomes relaxed and elongated through the process of relaxation and tension, in a practice of control and extension. The result is the aim of practice of boxing art: the mind, spirit and strength are accompanied by flowing and smoothing, with the body's attaining a good measure of relaxation and lengthening. This eliminates the effects of long term unnoticed tensions and pressures resulting from work. Moreover in case of apparent difficulties and mistakes, it adjusts a hunchbacked posture to an upright one.

The Ⅵ Form: Sequence of Holding with Linked Hands

【Preparation】Feet Together, Standing Tall

Same as Holding the Ball, Opening and Closing. (Fig 4-75)

【Gathering energy】

Stepping Out, Standing Tall to Bending the Knees, Holding the Ball. (Fig 4-76～Fig 4-78)

【Movement】

1. First sequence of Holding with Linked Hands (A)

Sink the shoulders as the legs rise, carrying the body up and erect. The arms follow the energy down, the hands have the *hukou* rounded. Using the wrists as an axis, rotate the wrists turning inward, then outward, turning the palms over. The little fingers now point upwards, the palms are turned forward, the fingers back and pointing to each other. The hands move outwards to the sides of the body in a natural arc. When they come level with the shoulders, the legs follow the energy into a squat. At the same time sink the elbows and relax the hip. The hands naturally slip lightly downwards to waist level, then move toward the front of the body and arc up as though carrying something in both hands to shoulder height. The little fingers touch at the sides, palms face up, fingers are extended and open as though "Holding in Linked Hands". (Fig 4-79～Fig 4-81)

2. Left sequence of Holding with Linked Hands

Bring the hands to face the chest as though carrying something back. The backs of the hands naturally turn to touch each other and then move to the sternum at center point. The hands move along the center line of the body downwards, arcing upwards and turning over the palms in front of the chest, so that the palms acing outward at *laogong* acupoint.

Turn the body to the left 90 degrees, pivoting on the left foot with the right foot toes gripping inward. Following the energy, pull the right foot forward. Arms and hands movement do not change. The center shifts back to the right leg. Sink the body, sit the hip. The left foot turns outwards, with the inner side of the sole touching the ground in an "empty" step. At the same time the body carries the hands and arms are carried outwards, the hands arcing to the sides pulling open to shoulder height. The left foot follows the energy with a big step forward, the center shifts over the left leg, the right foot follows it with a half-step, the inner sole touching the earth, the toes naturally turned out. At the. same time, sink the elbows and relax the hip, the hands naturally sink downwards. Then lightly extend the hands from the waist area toward the front of the body arcing upwards raising to shoulder height with the little fingers touching, the palms facing upwards, the palms and fingers open like carrying in linked hands. (Fig 4-82～Fig 4-87)

3. Right sequence of Holding with Linked Hands

The hands drop and extend forward, the right foot withdraws a half step; the center follows and shifts back, sit back on the right foot. The back of the hands touch and return inward to their position in front of the chest. At the same time, the left foot returns inwards, the toes lightly touching the ground making the left empty step. The hands rotate inward and extend palms-outward, again carried to their position in front of the chest. At the same time, the left foot moves outwards along the ground, and the center does not change. With the body as an axis, the left foot pivots and rotates inwards as the body turns right 90 degrees. With the body carrying the hands, the arms extend outwards. The center shifts to the left foot, as the body continues to turn. At the same time the hands follow the body's turning, arcing to the sides and extending, completing the right empty step. The right foot takes a big step forward, the center shifts to the forward leg, the back leg follows it with a half step, the inner sole following the ground, the toes naturally placed outwards. The hands follow the energy, moving down and then up to the front of the body completing the circle with palms together and forward at shoulder height, Holding with Linked Hands. (Fig 4-88~Fig 4-94)

4. Forward sequence, Holding with Linked Hands (B)

The hands slip down and extend forward, the left foot moves backwards. The center shifts back, the right foot's tiptoes touch the ground as in the right empty step. The right foot moves outward, following the ground as the center shifts to the left leg. The inside of the hands turn and are carried outward. The right foot pivots inward, the body turns left, the center shifts to the right, the hands pull open along the sides of the body. The center adjusts as the left foot moves to shoulder width. At the same time, the legs bend and sit, the hands carry the energy upwards, outwards, downwards, describing a circle, lightly extending from the waist and *hip* area towards the sides in a circle with the palms raised, as in the "Holding with Linked hands". (Fig 4-95~Fig 4-100)

5. Bend the knees hold the ball

The hands rotate inwards, gathering at the sternum, the backs of the fingers touching. They brush along the sides of the body, following the energy and slipping downward to the abdomen. Stand straight and raise the body, the arms following the energy outward, opening and separating. The thumbs point upward, the palms forward, strongly extending from the body and arcing energetically upward from the sides to the level of the shoulders. Bend the legs, sink the body, and sit at the same time the hands naturally face the chest and as in "Bending the Knees, Holding the Ball". (Fig 4-101~Fig 4-103)

6. Holding the ball, gathering the energy

The Same "Holding the Ball, opening and closing" and "Gathering Energy" form. (Fig 4-104~Fig 4-107)

【Notes】

When doing "Left Holding with Linked Hands," stiff or arthritic fingers, wrists, forearms and elbows will naturally rotate together. The hands will extend far forward from the chest, the arms slightly bent, palms and fingers comfortably extended and open, the waist and abdomen somewhat tucked, the pelvis tilted back so that the body is pulled upright and extended. The breath should coordinate with the movement of the forearms, the turning of the body, and execution of the steps backwards and forwards. When settling into the movement, the front knee should not extend beyond the toes. The mind and spirit are focused inwards yet also fully concentrated on the hands and fingers.

The gaze is directed naturally out into the distance from which it returns. The spirit and mind concentrate on the rotation of the fingers and changes in the inner organs. The organs relax, and the chest, following the qi, relaxes. The whole body from top to toe becomes harmonious.

【Significance】

"Carrying in Linked Hands" greatly helps the practitioner sense the circular and changing nature of the form through the movement of the body. The mind and spirit are drawn into the interior of the body, so that the whole body experiences complete rest. The Nine-form *taiji* Cao alternates relaxation and tension: if there is an opening out, there must be a coming together, if there is a gathering in, there must be a putting forth. It can also be an effective practice to gain fluid movement in stiff fingers, wrists, forearms and shoulders. It helps the body naturally engage in movements forward and back. It keeps the feet agile, as the whole body follows a smooth circular movement.

The Ⅶ Form: Spiral Winding

【Preparation】Feet Together, Standing Tall. (Fig 4-108)

【Gathering Energy】

"Stepping out, Standing Straight" to "Bending the Knees, Holding the Ball".

This sequence is the same as "Holding the ball, Opening and Closing". (Fig 4-109~Fig 4-111)

【Movement】

Right Spiral Winding Form

1. Right Spiral Winding: Weaving the Palms

Turn the body to the right; the center shifts to the left, the left hand still holds a ball as the body's angle doesn't change. At the same time the right palm faces upwards, following energy and returning to the front of the stomach. The right foot and toes touch the ground completing the Right Empty Step. Sit the hip, sink the body.

Take a big step with the right foot, the foot moving along the ground; the right knee extends forward. At the same time the right hand moves lightly along the right side of the body, then turns over and extends from the front of the body in an arc with the palm facing away from the body. Shift the center forward, pulling the left leg forward. This completes the Right Bow step. At the same time, the right hand moves towards the front, turning over, to reach the forearm straight ahead at shoulder height with the palm facing upwards. The left hand follows the energy and is near or touches the right inner elbow. (Fig 4-112~4-114)

2. Turn the Arm, Sit the body, Make Cloud Hands

Shift the center back, turn the feet, sink the body, and sit the hip. The palm of the right hand faces upwards, the arm moving in an arc from left to right in front of the forehead, making the Cloud Hands movement. (Fig 4-115)

3. Right Bow Step, Roll and Turn the Hands

The center shifts forward and the rear leg is pulled forward, making the Right Bow Step. At the same time the right hand is turned upward, and using the elbow as an axis continues circling toward the front, rolling and turning until the forearm is extended straight ahead. The left hand follows to touch the inner right elbow. (Fig 4-116)

4. Turn the Body, Wipe with Hands, Hold the Ball

Shift the center back, adjust the feet and sit back. Curl the right foot to the left, turning the body and using the body to carry the hands. The hands cross towards opposite sides of the body at the same level, as though to wipe open. The center shifts to the right leg, the body continues to turn left, using the hands to lead the body. The arms describe a circle. Adjust the left foot, following the energy, completing "Left Empty Sep, Holding the Ball". (Fig 4-117, Fig 4-118)

5. Left Bow Step, Wave Arms, Turn and Press

With the left leg facing forward, raise the foot and take a step. The center shifts forward, completing Left Bow Step. At the same time the left arm circles to the front waving outward to shoulder height. The palms face upward, the right hand follows the energy, touching or near the left inner elbow.

As the center shifts back, turn the foot and sit back, with the body following and turning left. Using the body to carry the hands, pull the forearm toward the body's left side circling back to the neck. At the same time sink the body and sit the hip, the left arm follows the energy, sinking the elbows. Rotate the hands, settle the waist; the center shifts forward, the left hand presses outward from the Bow Step. (Fig 4-119~Fig 4-121)

6. Left and Right Sides Bow Step, Raising the Hands

Right Raising: Sink the body, sit the hip. Using the energy, the body turns right. At the same time the right toes raise, and using the right heel as an axis, the foot turns outward. The center shifts right completing Right Side Bow Step. At the same time use the body to carry the hands and use the hands to lead the body. The right arm, extended, sinks downward toward the lower abdomen, then raises up toward the right side arcing upward to shoulder height, the tigers mouth *hu kou* facing upwards, the thumbs energetically upward, the left hand with the palm facing outward. (Fig 4-122)

Left movement: The body shifts left, completing Left Bow Step. At the same time the left hand rotates the arm like a needle, moving it up, then down, then moving from left to right, in an arc. Lightly move the arm to the front of the lower abdomen, then briskly return it to at shoulder height. The right arm is still extended, the knees rising but still bent. (Fig 4-123, Fig 4-124)

7. Bend Knees Hold the Ball

The body briefly leans back, using the hands and small joints to pull the arms outwards towards the back. Use the momentum of the arms to return to the front so that the hands end up facing the chest holding the ball. With the energy of the right leg, very lightly gather it a half step inwards to shoulder's width, completing Bend Knee Hold the Ball. (Fig 4-125)

8. Hold the Ball Gather Energy

The same as Holding the Ball, Opening and Closing form and Holding the Ball Gathering Energy.

Left Spiral Winding Form

Left Spiral Winding form is the same as Right Spiral Winding Form, but on opposite side. (Fig 4-126~Fig 4-143)

【Notes】

All the movements should link up naturally; there should be no stops or breaks in continuity. Notice and experience the movement through the energy of sinking the body and the sitting the *kua*. Use the movement of the torso as an axis and to provide strength to carry the movement of the arms, waist, and twisting of the legs. The body movements are circular and natural, relaxed, light, open and extended. The powerful breath becomes open and natural.

【Significance】

Spiral Winding Form derives from traditional martial arts body work: the practice of foot work, hand work and energy work. The limbs' spiral winding and the body's twisting and turning coordinates the whole body in the natural execution of all the movements. The form can make one's foundation agile yet stable. It can raise the mind, spirit, and strength. The form encompasses both order and change. It confers the ability to "raise a hand and look around to the four directions, then move a step and take care of 8 places."

The Ⅷ Form: Peaceful Spirit Supports The Foundation

【Preparation】Feet Together, Standing Tall. The movement is like "Holding the Ball, opening and closing". (Fig 4-144)

【Gathering Energy】: "Stepping out, Standing Tall" to "Bending the Knees, Holding the Ball". The movement is like "Holding the Ball, Opening and Closing". (Fig 4-145~Fig 4-147)

1. Pressing Down in front of the Abdomen

The hands face the chest, then rotate to face downward, palms down, fingers opposed. Press downwards until they reach the abdomen. Concentrate the spirit and grasp the *qi*; the mind stays in the *dantian*. (Fig 4-148)

2. Bending the Knees, Hands Move Back

The waist and back briefly lean back, the hands move forward and outward in an arc, standing straight, with the body rising. The hands continue to circle the waist, moving around the body to the back in an arc, until they reach the lower spine, where they lightly touch just outside of the tailbone and area outside of the *ming men*, the fingers naturally meeting. At the same time bring the arms back, bend the knees and sit. (Fig 4-149, Fig 4-150)

3. Return to Front of Abdomen and Press Lightly

Briefly sink the body, at the same time the tail bone area relaxes and opens. The body is drawn upwards, standing straight. The shoulder and neck area and the spine relax. The hands move downwards, and naturally slipping to the sides of the body, then from the sides springing up lightly to shoulder level. The hands move forward, naturally coming together as though holding a ball.

Sit the hip, relax the energy in the waist and again press down until the hands are in front of the abdomen. Relax the shoulders and hands, sink the body and grasp the *qi*, the heels naturally firm on the ground, and the spirit is concentrated in the *dan tian* (Fig 4-151, Fig 4-152).

4. Gather the Energy

The hands, in front of the abdomen, press down towards the sides in an arcing motion, using the energy of the earth to raise the body, moving into "Stepping Out, Standing Tall". The left foot moves toward the right foot, returning to the starting position, "Feet Together, Standing Tall". (Fig 4-153, Fig 4-154)

【Notes】

The heart is calm, the qi is tranquil, and mind and spirit are recollected. This is "Peaceful Spirit Supports the Foundation." In this movement, the shoulders, arms, and hands relax. The breath is deep, long, fine and even. The whole body naturally relaxes, and the mind protects the dan tian.

【Significance】

Practicing "Peaceful Spirit Supports the Foundation" can encourage the qi in the dan tian to move in a circular motion, help the waist area relax, and the breath to deepen and lengthen. When the waist and abdomen are interconnected, the inner qi of the dan tian can follow the deepening of the breath. The body relaxes and is pervaded with peacefulness. In this way the movement helps the body recover the primordial *qi*, bringing a peaceful spirit and a light heart.

The IX Form: Relax the Heart, Lessen the Load

【Preparation】Feet Together, Standing Tall

This is the same movement as "Holding the Ball, Opening and Closing". (Fig 4-155)

【Gather the Energy】

"Stepping out, Standing Tall" to "Bending Knees, Holding the Ball"

This is the same movement as "Holding the Ball, Opening and Closing" (Fig 4-156~Fig 4-158)

【Movement】

1. Raise the Arms and Press the Palms; Stand Straight and Raise the Body

Rotate the wrists and raise the hands until they reach shoulder height. Sink the elbows and sit the wrists, sink the body and press the hands down until they reach the area in front of the abdomen. stand straight and raise the body. (Fig 4-159~Fig 4-161)

2. Turn over the Hands, Brush with Palms; Relax the Heart and Lessen the Load

The forearms rotate inward so that the backs of the hands touch each other. The fingers face down, the palms face out. Raise the arms and raise the shoulders, and raising the chest, inhale *qi*. The *hukou* and thumb follow the body's center line from below to above, pulling upward, until it reaches the chest area. Then the hands turn over and outwards, rotating the wrists and turning over the palms so that the fingers point upwards, the backs of the hand touching. They swiftly move down along the sternum, hands brushing lightly downward as though brushing off dust and dirt. The inner organs and the muscles and flesh of the whole body relax thoroughly, following the movement. At the same time the *qi* pours out, and the whole body has a feeling of letting go of a heavy load. (Fig 4-162~Fig 4-164)

Follow the energy, bend the knees, and hold the ball. The body stands straight, the hand rotate inward, the arms move forward rising to shoulder height. Sink the elbows and sit the wrists, the arms follow the energy naturally slipping down to the sides of the body. The body center is straight and extended, the mind and spirit relaxed. Again they hands move down and then with the fingers touching, rising and then lightly brushing off with the palms. Sink the body as the arms open outward, following the energy, again gather it in while pressing downward toward the front of the abdomen. (Fig 4-165~Fig 4-172)

3. Gathering the Energy

As the body reaches full height, the hands trace along the body from the front to the sides, sinking down to the lower abdomen then out to the sides, reaching the *hip* in a circling motion. Return to the starting form "Feet together, Standing Straight". (Fig 4-173, Fig 4-174)

【Notes】

Fully inhale *qi*, fully exhale *qi*. The inner organs, muscles and flesh completely relax. The spirit and mind thoroughly relax, the body is completely extended, with all tension and pressure released into the ground. After gathering energy for the last time, continue to regulate the breath. Then the body will move lightly and naturally with the attention focused inward. The body and heart will be light and stable.

> 【Significance】
> Practicing "Relax the Heart, Lessen the Load" helps the shoulder, neck and chest areas and the all the inner muscles to let go. The body's tensions and pressures from top to toe are absorbed into the ground.
> The whole body feels relaxed, the heart is light and happy, and the spirit comfortable with a feeling that all burdens have been released.

第五章　简化太极拳套路

> 本章主要介绍二十四式太极拳。二十四式太极拳是目前流传较广、深受群众喜爱的太极拳套路。本章通过清晰详尽的文字说明和图片展示，将二十四式太极拳的动作逐一分开讲解，每一式的动作方法、动作要点、易犯错误以及纠正方法都做了细致的阐述，便于习练者充分到位地掌握二十四式太极拳的内涵与精髓。

一、起势

1. 准备姿势

身体自然直立，两脚并拢，两臂自然下垂，两手放在大腿外侧，手指微屈。头颈正直，下颌微收，口微闭，舌抵上腭，胸腹放松，注意力集中，眼向前平视。如图5-1所示。

2. 动作方法

左脚向左分开半步，两脚间距离与肩同宽，成开立步，两脚平行。如图5-2所示。

图 5-1

图 5-2

两臂慢慢向前平举，两手与肩同高，手心向下，指尖向前，肘关节向下微屈。如图5-3所示。

上体保持正直，两腿屈膝下蹲，身体重心均衡地落在两腿之间，同时两掌轻轻下按，两肘下垂与两膝相对，眼平视前方。如图5-4、图5-5所示。

3. 动作要点

（1）并步站立和开立步时，两脚平行，身体重心落在两脚之间。

（2）由并步转换成开立步时，首先左膝放松，右膝自然微屈，身体重心便过渡到右腿上，然后左脚轻轻提起向左旁开半步，落地是左脚尖先着地，随身体重心左移慢慢过渡到全脚掌踩实地面。体现出太极拳"点起点落、轻起轻落"的特点。

图 5-3

图 5-4

图 5-5

（3）手臂前举时，两手先在体侧将掌心转向后方再慢慢向前平举，腕关节保持适度紧张，不要过分松软。

（4）下按到位时两手在腹部前面，按掌到终点时舒展手掌和手指。

（5）上体保持正直，不能前俯后仰。尽量保持脊背、臀部和脚跟在同一个垂直面上；无论两臂前举或是下按，两肘尖都不能外展上扬，两肩不能紧张、耸起。

4. 易犯错误

身体僵硬，挺胸或身体不能保持中正，双臂向下按掌时太用力。

5. 纠正方法

尽量体会身体放松的状态或靠意念帮助自己放松，做到含胸拔背敛臀；双臂下按时注意双臂用力的顺序，沉肩坠肘再塌腕按掌。

二、左、右野马分鬃

1. 左野马分鬃动作方法

身体微向右转，重心移至右腿上，同时右手收在胸前平屈，手心向下，左手经提前向右下划弧放在右手下，手心向上，呈抱球状，左脚随之收到右腿内侧，脚尖点地，眼看右手。如图5-6、图5-7所示。

上体左转，左脚向左前方迈出，脚跟轻轻点地，身体重心仍在右腿。

重心前移，左脚踏实，左腿屈膝前弓成左弓步，右脚跟向外碾动。同时左右手慢慢分别向左上、右下分开，左手高与眼平，肘微屈。右手落在右胯旁，手心向下，指尖向前，眼看左手。如图 5-8～图 5-10 所示。

2. 右野马分鬃动作方法

上体慢慢后坐,重心移到右腿上,左脚尖翘起,微向外撇。如图 5-11 所示。

随后左腿慢慢前弓,身体左转,重心再移到左腿上,同时左手翻转向下,收在胸前平屈,右手向左上划弧放在左手下,两手心相对成抱球状。如图 5-12 所示。

上体稍右转,右脚随之收到左脚内侧,脚尖点地,眼看左手。如图 5-13 所示。

右腿向右前方迈出,左脚跟后蹬,成右弓步。同时左右手分别慢慢向左下、右上分开,右手高与眼平,肘关节微屈。如图 5-14～图 5-16 所示。

第二个左野马分鬃的做法与右野马分鬃的做法相同,只是方向相反。如图 5-17～图 5-22 所示。

图 5-6

图 5-7

图 5-8

图 5-9

图 5-10

图 5-11

图 5-12　　　　　　　图 5-13　　　　　　　图 5-14

图 5-15　　　　　　　图 5-16　　　　　　　图 5-17

图 5-18　　　　　　　图 5-19　　　　　　　图 5-20

图 5-21

图 5-22

3. 动作要点

(1) 转体与抱球要协调同步地完成,抱球时右臂要适度放松,高度大致与肩平,肩部放松,手指微屈,肘略低与肩,腕略低于手,前臂与胸间要留有 20~30 厘米的距离,整个右臂呈弧形。左手翻掌划弧伴随前臂的向外旋转。

(2) 左脚或右脚收至支撑脚内侧,脚尖点地以增加身体的平衡性,此时身体重心绝大部分落在支撑腿上,随着动作熟练及身体控制能力的增强,内收的脚可以不点地而直接上步。

(3) 无论左脚或右脚向前上步,身体重心仍然要稳定在支撑腿上,否则会因身体重心的过早前移使身体失去平衡而出现"跨步"现象,应该是上步脚脚跟落地后,身体重心再缓慢过渡到前面。保持两脚横向距离在 10~30 厘米左右。

(4) 弓步完成是膝盖与脚尖应该上下对正,其连线与地面垂直。弓步时后腿不能挺直,否则会造成腰胯紧张,也不能太屈,形成松软无力的现象,应该自然伸直,脚跟踏实地面。弓步时身体重心分配的比例是前腿约承担三分之二,后腿约承担三分之一。

(5) 分手时手心斜向上,力点在前臂外侧,向左或右斜上方"靠"出。此时肩部要松沉,肘部微屈,分到顶点时要舒展掌指,体现出由轻灵转向沉稳的气势。向下分开的手要捋至胯关节旁,手心向下,指尖向前,肘关节微屈,动作到位时要做到舒展掌指,坐腕、沉肩。

(6) 注意动作与眼神的配合。起势时眼看前方,做野马分鬃时应随手的屈收合抱和分靠动作运用眼神,避免低头或左顾右盼。

(7) 野马分鬃转换时,身体重心起伏幅度不大,要基本保持平稳,转体撇脚时身体重心也要平稳匀缓后移;收脚时重心前移,待支撑腿稳定后再以大腿的力量把后脚提收起来,否则会出现蹬踏地面或拖擦地面的现象。

注意:上体不要前俯后仰,两手分开要保持弧形,身体转动要以腰为轴,做弓步与分手的速度要一致。

4. 易犯错误

身体各部位在转动时用力不连贯;弓步后腿脚尖不相随,不适当内扣导致弓步合髋不够横裆开胯;弓步时双脚在一条线上。

5. 纠正方法

原地体会以腰带臂的整体顺畅的左右转动；原地体会弓步动作中，绷直的后腿脚跟向外碾动及脚尖内扣的动作；顺弓步时两脚间的横向距离不能少于 30 厘米。

三、白鹤亮翅

1. 动作方法

上体微向左转，重心前移右脚向前跟步，前脚掌轻落于左脚后，相距约一脚长，两手翻转抱球，左手在上，眼看左手。如图 5-23 所示。

身体重心后移，右脚踏实，上体后坐的同时微向右转，两手交错分开，右手上举，左手下落，眼看右手。如图 5-24 所示。

左脚提起稍前点成左虚步，右手在右额侧前掌心向左，左手翻掌向下按在左腿旁，上体扭正，眼平视前方。如图 5-25 所示。

图 5-23　　　　　　　　图 5-24　　　　　　　　图 5-25

2. 动作要领

（1）做跟步时右脚前脚掌轻轻落地并外展约 45 度，以便为下一步的虚步做好铺垫。

（2）步伐转换时，强调腰部参与旋转的运动，跟步时腰部微向左转，合胯收脚，后坐时腰部微右转，身体重心后移。

（3）随着两手上下分开，注意下颌微收，头微上顶，配合吸气；两手分至顶点时右手外展，左手下按，配合呼气下沉、松腰松胯、精神集中。

3. 易犯错误

虚步时虚实不够分明，身体前倾或后仰；右手上扬太高。

4. 纠正方法

虚步时身体几乎 90% 的重量由后腿承受；右手应上扬至右额前方，不能举过头顶。

四、左、右搂膝拗步

1. 动作方法

（1）左搂膝拗步。

上体稍左转，右手掌心翻转向上摆至体前。如图 5-26 所示。

上体右转，右手经体前向左向下划弧摆至右后方，同时左手随身体右转向上经脸前向右划弧落在右肩前，掌心向下，左脚收在右脚内侧，脚尖点地。头随体转，眼看右手。

上体稍左转，左脚向左前方迈出一步，脚跟落地，同时右臂屈肘收在头侧，虎口朝向头部，掌心斜向前，左手落在腹前。眼看前方。如图 5-27～图 5-29 所示。

上体继续向左转动，身体重心缓慢前移；左脚慢慢踏实成左弓步，后腿自然蹬直；左手从左膝上方搂过停在左腿外侧，掌心向下，指尖向前，右手从头侧直接向前推出，掌高与鼻平，掌心向前，五指向上，沉肩坠肘；眼看右掌。如图 5-30 所示。

（2）右搂膝拗步。

身体重心稍向后移，上体左转同时左脚尖外撇，两臂划弧开始摆动；右手屈肘回收，掌心向下，左手翻掌向上在腹前下方。如图 5-31 所示。

图 5-26

图 5-27

图 5-28

图 5-29

图 5-30

图 5-31

上体左转，重心前移，左脚踏实，右脚收到左脚内侧，脚尖点地；右手经头前划弧摆至左肩前，掌心向下，左手向左上方划弧上举，与头同高，掌心向上；眼看左手。如图 5-32、图 5-33 所示。

上体稍右转；右脚向前迈出一步，脚跟落地；左臂屈肘，左手收至肩上，右手落至腹前；眼看前方。如图 5-34 所示。

图 5-32

图 5-33

图 5-34

上体继续右转，重心前移；右脚踏实，右腿屈弓成右弓步；右手经右膝上方搂过停于右腿外侧，掌心向下，指尖向前，左手向前推出与鼻尖同高，掌心向前，指尖向上；眼看左手。如图 5-35 所示。

左搂膝拗步与前式相同。如图 5-36～5-40 所示。

图 5-35

图 5-36

图 5-37

图 5-38

图 5-39

图 5-40

2. 动作要领

(1) 搂膝拗步练习时要以腰部的转动带动四肢,突出太极拳以腰为轴的特点。

(2) 做搂推动作时前推、下搂的两掌和弓腿应同时到位,不分先后;当推掌到终点时,虎口撑圆,放松掌指,沉肩坠肘,把意念集中在五指和掌根上,同时配合呼气实腹。

(3) 注意手推出后身体不前俯后仰,要松腰松胯,推掌时沉肩垂肘。坐腕舒掌,必须松腰弓腿上下协调一致,弓步时两脚横向距离不少于 30 厘米。

3. 易犯错误

转体摆臂时腰部转动太多或手臂动作幅度过大;搂推时下搂掌和前推掌不协调同步;弓步时双脚在一条直线上。

4. 纠正方法

腰部微左转或右转,下划臂时高不过头,低不过小腹;搂推时注意用腰部的转动来带动全身协调用力;拗弓步两脚跟横向距离保持在 20~30 厘米。

五、手挥琵琶

1. 动作方法

右脚向前跟进半步,右臂稍向前伸展,手臂及腕关节放松。如图 5-41 所示。

上体后坐,身体重心移至右腿上,上体微右转;右手屈肘后引,左手向左向上划弧摆至体前。如图 5-42 所示。

上体稍左转,左脚略提起稍向前移,变成左虚步,两臂沉肘合抱于体前;左手掌心向右,高与鼻平,右手掌心向左与左肘相对;眼看左手。如图 5-43 所示。

2. 动作要点

(1) 后坐引手时,左手前摆和右手后引的动作与身体重心后移、上体右转等协调一致完成。

(2) 合抱定势时,肩关节不能夹紧身体,两臂应保持弧形,充分掤展,肘部不能过分弯曲或伸直。同时做到顶头沉肩,上体中正,呼气下沉,松胸实腹。

图 5-41

图 5-42

图 5-43

3. 易犯错误

虚步时重心分配不合理,身体前倾或后仰;合手时两臂夹臂向下。

4. 纠正方法

体会虚步时身体重心的合理分配;突出虚步合手时左肘内夹外旋和右手下推外旋至左肘下方的动作,体会左臂夹肘抱掌与右臂下推抱掌的合劲。

六、左、右倒卷肱

1. 动作方法

(1) 右倒卷肱。

上体稍右转,两手翻掌向上,右手向下经腰侧划弧至右后方,略比肩高,左手在体前平举;头随体转,眼看右手。如图 5-44、图 5-45 所示。

上体稍左转,左脚提起后退一步,脚前掌着地;右臂屈收在肩上耳侧,掌心向前下方;眼看左手。如图 5-46 所示。

图 5-44

图 5-45

图 5-46

上体继续左转，身体重心后移至左脚上；右脚脚跟提起扭正方向，右膝微屈成右虚步；右手推至体前，腕高与肩平，掌心向前，左手向下、向后划弧收在腰侧；眼看右手。如图 5-47 所示。

（2）左倒卷肱。

左倒卷肱与右倒卷肱动作相同，方向相反。如图 5-48～图 5-50 所示。

右倒卷肱与前式相同。如图 5-51～图 5-53 所示。

左倒卷肱与前式相同。如图 5-54～图 5-56 所示。

2．动作要点

（1）退步时支撑腿完全支撑身体重量后才能提收另一脚，脚尖自然下垂，不超过支撑脚脚踝高度；提起的脚要先向后再微向左或右侧后方点地，注意脚尖外展，保证步幅、落地、方向正确，身体不偏不倒，起伏不大，两腿虚实分明。

（2）前推时手不要伸直，后手不要直线回收，仍走弧线，前推时要转腰松胯，与两手速度一致，避免僵硬。退步时脚尖着地再慢慢踏实，同时把前脚扭正。退左脚稍向左后斜，退右脚稍向右后斜，避免两脚在前后一条线上。

图 5-47

图 5-48

图 5-49

图 5-50

图 5-51

图 5-52

图 5-53

图 5-54

图 5-55

图 5-56

（3）眼神应先随转体向侧看，然后再转看前手。

3. 易犯错误

转体撤手时，两臂呈直线；后撤步时后撤脚重心过渡不正确；后撤步时两脚落在一条直线上使胯部过紧出现夹裆。

4. 纠正方法

转体撤手时手走弧线，以腰带臂圆活自然；后撤步时重心平稳放在支撑腿上；后撤脚要略微偏左或偏右落地。

七、左揽雀尾

1. 动作方法

上体微向右转；右手由腰侧向右后上方划弧平举高与肩平，掌心向上，左手在体前下落，手心向下；头随体转；眼看右手。如图 5-57 所示。

上体继续右转；右手屈抱于右胸前，掌心向下，左手划弧下落屈抱于腹前，掌心翻转向上，两手成抱球状；同时左脚收到右脚内侧，脚尖点地；眼看右手。如图 5-58、图 5-59 所示。

图 5-57　　　　　　　　图 5-58　　　　　　　　图 5-59

上体左转；左脚向前迈出一步，脚跟着地。如图 5-60 所示。

上体继续左转，身体重心前移；左脚踏实成左弓步，右腿自然蹬直；两手前后分开，左臂弧形向前掤架，高与肩平，右手向下划弧至右胯旁按掌，掌心向下，指尖向前；眼看左前臂。如图 5-61 所示。

上体微向左转；左手向左前方伸展，掌心转向下，右手转成掌心向上经腹前向上、向前摆至左前臂内侧；眼看左手。如图 5-62 所示。

图 5-60　　　　　　　　图 5-61　　　　　　　　图 5-62

上体右转，身体重心后移落在右腿上；左腿自然伸直；两手同时向下经腹前向右后方划弧，右手停于侧后方与头同高，左臂平屈于胸前，掌心向内；眼看右手。如图 5-63、图 5-64 所示。

上体左转面向前方;右臂屈肘收在胸前,右手搭在左前臂内侧,掌心向前,指尖向上;眼看前方。如图5-65所示。

图 5-63

图 5-64

图 5-65

身体重心前移;左腿屈弓成左弓步;右手推送左前臂向体前挤出,与肩同高,两臂撑圆;眼看前方。如图5-66所示。

上体后坐,身体重心移至右腿上;左脚尖翘起,左手翻转向下,右手经左腕上方向前向右划弧分开与肩同宽,屈肘后引收至腹前;眼向前平视。如图5-67、图5-68所示。

图 5-66

图 5-67

图 5-68

身体重心前移;左脚踏实成左弓步;两手弧线推至体前与肩同高,掌心向前,指尖向上;眼看前方。如图5-69、图5-70所示。

2. 动作要点

(1) 上下肢要协调配合,掤、捋、挤、按要与弓腿协调一致,捋和引手与屈腿后坐一致,上体中正。

(2) 注意动作的连贯性和身体重心的虚实转换,做到拳势之间既有虚实转换,又要连续衔接。

（3）弓步时两脚横向距离不超过10厘米，两腿屈伸要灵活，避免身体出现高低起伏的现象。

（4）下捋时两臂要与腰部旋转协调一致；前挤时转体与搭手同时完成，挤出后两肩松沉，两臂撑圆，上体正直，不俯身突臀；后坐时左腿膝部不要挺直，按掌时两手沿弧线向上向前按出。

图 5-69

图 5-70

3. 易犯错误

身体重心不稳，出现起伏；捋时腰部转动幅度过大，转腰与下捋不能协调一致，转腰快而下捋慢；转体搭手时双手高过头顶再回身完成挤势；按掌时前脚尖不翘起，两手距离过大。

4. 纠正方法

动作中以腰带动整个动作完成，两腿屈伸要灵活自如，避免出现身体忽高忽低的现象；捋的动作完成时，同腰转动方向的手平举稍高于肩与正前方成130°角；按掌时重心充分后坐，前脚尖翘起，双手分开与肩宽，屈肘，两手划弧线后引至胸前，下按至小腹再向前推出。

八、右揽雀尾

动作方法

身体重心后移，上体右转；左脚尖内扣，右手经头前划弧右摆，两手平举于身体两侧，掌心向外。如图5-71、图5-72所示。

重心左移；左腿屈，右脚收到左脚内侧，脚尖点地；两手在胸前成抱球状，左手在上，右手在下；眼看左手。如图5-73、图5-74所示。

转体上步（如图5-75所示）、弓步掤臂（如图5-76所示）、转体摆臂（如图5-77所示）、转体后捋（如图5-78所示）、转体搭手（如图5-79、图5-80所示）、弓步前挤（如图5-81所示）、后坐引手（如图5-82～图5-84所示）、弓步按掌（如图5-85所示）的动作与左揽雀尾相同，只是方向相反。

图 5-71

图 5-72

图 5-73

图 5-74

图 5-75

图 5-76

图 5-77

图 5-78

图 5-79

图 5-80　　　　　图 5-81　　　　　图 5-82

图 5-83　　　　　图 5-84　　　　　图 5-85

九、单鞭

1. 动作方法

重心左移，上体左转；右脚尖内扣；两臂交叉向左运转，左手经头前向左划弧至身体左侧，掌心向外，右手经腹前向左划弧至左肋前，掌心向上；眼神随左手移动。如图 5-86、图 5-87 所示。

上体右转，重心右移；左脚收到右脚内侧脚尖点地；右手向右划弧经头前至身体右前方成勾手，手腕与肩同高，左手向下向右划弧，经腹前至右肩前，掌心向内；眼神随右手转移，看勾手。如图 5-88、图 5-89 所示。

上体左转；左脚向左前方上步，脚跟点地；左手经脸前向左划弧，掌心向内；眼看左手。如图 5-90 所示。

身体重心前移；左脚踏实成左弓步，右腿自然蹬直，脚跟外展；左手经脸前翻掌向前推出，左臂与左腿上下相对；眼看左手。如图 5-91 所示。

图 5-86

图 5-87

图 5-88

图 5-89

图 5-90

图 5-91

2．动作要点

（1）弓步方向应略向左前方，不超过 30°角，两脚宽约 10 厘米。

（2）推掌时随上体左转，左腿前弓，左手边翻掌边向前推出，推掌完成时，要松腰、松胯、沉腕、展掌、舒指。

3．易犯错误

左手推掌时绕腕，形成"腕花"；两臂展开过大成直线或成 90°；勾手手臂太直或太屈；下肢弓步与推掌不同步，出现弓步到位后推掌还没有完成；弓时两腿在一条直线或左脚落于右脚的右侧使髋拧紧夹胯。

4．纠正方法

控制好左手翻掌的时机，不要翻掌太晚，左掌随重心移动，边移动边翻腕，等翻腕完成正好随下肢之势推出；尽量保持两臂角度在 130°左右；勾手臂注意做到沉肩坠肘塌腕；伴随重心前移翻手推掌,做到弓步和推掌同时完成;弓步时左右脚横向距离保持在10~15厘米,左脚落于右脚的左侧。

十、云手

1. 动作方法

身体重心后移,上体右转;左脚尖内扣;左手向下划弧经腹前至右肩前,掌心向内,右手勾手松开成掌,掌心向外;眼看右手。如图5-92、图5-93所示。

上体左转,重心左移;右脚向左脚收拢,脚前掌先着地,然后全脚踏实,两腿屈膝半蹲,两脚相距10厘米平行开立;左手经头前向左划弧运转,掌心向外翻转至身体左侧,与肩部同高,右手向下经腹前向左划弧至左肩前方,掌心转向内;眼随手走。如图5-94~图5-96所示。

上体右转,身体重心移向右腿;左脚向左横开一步,脚前掌先落地后全脚落地;右手经头前向右划弧运转,掌心由内逐渐转向外,停于身体右侧,与肩部同高,左掌下落经腹前向右划弧至右肩前,掌心渐翻向内;眼随手运转。如图5-97~图5-99所示。

图 5-92

图 5-93

图 5-94

图 5-95

图 5-96

图 5-97

图 5-98　　　　　　　　　图 5-99　　　　　　　　　图 5-100

图 5-101　　　　　　　　图 5-102　　　　　　　　图 5-103

图 5-104　　　　　　　　图 5-105　　　　　　　　图 5-106

左云收脚（如图 5-100、图 5-101 所示）、右云开步（如图 5-102～图 5-104 所示）、左云收脚（如图 5-105、图 5-106 所示）动作与前面相同。

2．动作要点

（1）云手动作要做到以腰为轴，转腰带手，身手合一。

（2）本式步法是侧行步，注意点起点落、轻起轻落，步幅要合度，上体不可左歪右扭。

（3）两手交错向左右划立圆，同时旋臂翻掌。

3．易犯错误

侧行步时，两脚尖外撇成八字形或呈弓步状侧行；腰部转动太大；双臂划弧时动作路线太大；侧行步和手臂动作不协调配合。

4．纠正方法

加强对仆步正确动作要领的了解并反复练习，做到仆步腿的脚尖内扣，膝部伸直，支撑腿全脚着地，臀部下沉，身体稍微前倾；独立时，由仆步屈膝，靠后退蹬地帮助完成到弓步的转变，并伴随重心充分前移，直至把重心过渡到前面的腿上，后腿能轻灵干净地提起。

十一、单鞭

1．动作方法

上体右转，重心移在右腿上，左脚跟提起，右手经头前向右划弧至右前方翻转成勾手；左手向下经腹前向右划弧至右肩前，掌心转向内；眼看勾手。如图 5-107～图 5-109 所示。

上体稍左转，左脚向左前方上步，脚跟落地，左手经面前向左划弧，掌心向内；眼看左手。如图 5-110 所示。

上体继续左转，身体重心前移，左脚踏实，成左弓步，左手经面前翻转向前推出，高与肩平；眼看左手。如图 5-111 所示。

图 5-107

图 5-108

图 5-109

图 5-110

图 5-111

2. 动作要点

易犯错误及纠正方法同云手前的单鞭。

十二、高探马

1. 动作方法

后脚向前收拢半步距前脚一脚长，脚前掌着地；右勾手松开，两手翻转向上，两臂前后平举，肘关节微屈；眼看左手。如图 5-112 所示。

上体稍右转，身体重心后移，右脚踏实，右腿屈坐，左脚跟提起；右臂弯曲，右手卷收至头侧，眼平视前方。如图 5-113 所示。

上体左转，右肩前送，左脚提起前点，脚前掌着地成左虚步；右手从头侧向前推出，高与头平。如图 5-114 所示。

图 5-112

图 5-113

图 5-114

2. 动作要点

本式前推的掌高与头平,后手要收至腹前。

3. 易犯错误

虚步时点腿太直或过虚,身体前倾或后仰;左手收到左腰侧。

4. 纠正方法

体会虚步时两腿承担身体重量的虚实比例,并保持好身体的基本形态姿势,不挺胸收腹突臀;左肘收于腰侧,左手收至腹前。

十三、右蹬脚

1. 动作方法

上体稍向左转,左脚向后提收再向左前方上步,脚跟落地;右手稍向后收,左手经右手手臂上方穿出,两手腕关节相交,左掌掌心斜向上,右掌掌心斜向下;眼看左手。如图5-115、图5-116所示。

左脚踏实,身体重心前移成左弓步,上体稍向右转,两手向两侧划弧分开,掌心向外。如图5-117所示。

图 5-115

图 5-116

图 5-117

右脚收至左脚内侧,脚尖点地;两手向腹前划弧合抱于胸前,右手在外,两掌心都向内;眼看右前方。如图5-118所示。

两手翻转向右前方和左后方划弧分开撑于两侧,掌心向外,腕部与肩平;左腿支撑,右腿屈膝上提,脚跟用力慢慢向前上方蹬出,右腿与右臂上下相对;眼看右手。如图5-119、图5-120所示。

2. 动作要点

(1)两手合抱要保持两肩松沉、两肘微坠,两臂抱圆;两手划弧分开时不要超过头部高度。

(2) 支撑腿完全支撑身体重量后再提膝蹬脚。

整个动作注意穿掌与上步一致、弓腿与分手一致、收脚与抱手一致、蹬脚与分手撑臂一致。

图 5-118　　　　　　　　图 5-119　　　　　　　　图 5-120

3. 易犯错误

蹬脚时，支撑腿不稳，身体后仰或前倾弯腰；蹬脚时手脚方向不一致，两臂分掌过大，一高一低；蹬脚时没有勾脚尖，蹬脚腿太直或太屈。

4. 纠正方法

精神放松，不追求蹬脚高度，加强腿部柔韧性练习，加强腿部力量练习，提高身体的控制能力；蹬脚时强调蹬脚腿与同侧手方向一致，力达脚跟，腿自然微屈，蹬脚时同侧臂腿的肩与髋、肘与膝相对，两臂腕部与肩同高；蹬脚动作与两手翻掌外撑协调一致，蹬脚到位时，做到肘部微屈，沉肩、塌腕、舒掌。

十四、双峰贯耳

1. 动作方法

屈膝并手：右小腿屈膝收回，脚尖自然下垂，左手向前向下划弧与右手并行落在右膝上方，掌心向上；眼看前方。如图 5-121 所示。

上步收手：右脚下落向右前方上步，脚跟着地，脚尖斜向右前方，两手收至腰侧，掌心向上。如图 5-122 所示。

弓步贯拳：身体重心前移，右脚踏实成右弓步，两手握拳从两侧向上、向前划弧摆至头前，两臂半屈成钳形，两拳相对，相距同头宽，两臂内旋，拳眼斜向下。眼看前方。如图 5-123 所示。

2. 动作要点

(1) 贯拳力点在拳面，身体中正，沉肩坠肘。

(2) 握拳不能过于紧张，也不能拳心松空。

图 5-121

图 5-122

图 5-123

3. 易犯错误

右脚落地即成弓步;贯拳时双臂太直或太高,低头;贯拳时双手出现"绕手腕";弓步与贯拳动作不协调,完成动作不是同时到位,弓步成形后还有双臂慢慢上举贯打的现象。

4. 纠正方法

注意右脚落地时右脚跟先落地,重心仍在左脚;两臂成弧形钳状,两拳相距与头宽,两臂内旋,拳眼斜向下置于头前,眼看前方;由掌变拳动作是两手由膝侧继续划弧下落经过腰侧时,前臂内旋逐渐握拳,靠手臂内旋带动双拳呈钳形而不是手臂不内旋只是屈腕让拳绕腕一圈来完成;完成动作时,有意识控制动作速度,使上下肢同时协调到位。

十五、转身左蹬脚

1. 动作方法

重心渐渐移至左腿上,上体左转,右脚尖里扣,两拳松开,左手随转体经头前向左划弧,两手平举于身体两侧;眼看左手。如图 5-124、图 5-125 所示。

图 5-124

图 5-125

图 5-126

重心再移至右腿上，右腿屈膝后坐，左脚收至右脚内侧，脚尖点地，同时两手由外圈向里圈划弧合抱于胸前，左手在外，手心均向后；眼看前方。如图5-126、图5-127所示。

两手向左前方和右后方划弧分开，撑举在身体两侧；左脚提起向左前方慢慢蹬出，左臂与左腿上下相对；眼看左手。如图5-128、图5-129所示。

图 5-127

图 5-128

图 5-129

2. 动作要点

（1）左蹬脚与右蹬脚的方向要对称。
（2）其他要点与右蹬脚相同。

十六、左下式独立

1. 动作方法

左腿收回平屈，左脚脚尖向下自然垂于右腿内侧，上体右转；右手五指捏拢成勾手，左手经头前划弧摆至右肩前，掌心向右；眼看勾手。如图5-130、图5-131所示。

图 5-130

图 5-131

图 5-132

右腿屈蹲,左脚向左侧旁开一步,脚前掌先着地后再慢慢过渡到全脚掌落地,左腿伸直;右手落于右肋前;眼看勾手。如图 5-132、图 5-133 所示。

身体重心降低,右腿屈膝全蹲,上体左转成左仆步;左手沿左腿内侧向左穿掌,掌心向前,指尖向左;眼看左手。如图 5-134 所示。

身体重心慢慢移向左腿,左脚脚尖外撇,左腿屈膝前弓成左弓步;右腿自然伸直,脚尖内扣;左手继续前穿向上挑起,右手前臂内旋背于身后,勾尖朝上;眼看左手。如图 5-135 所示。

图 5-133

图 5-134

图 5-135

上体左转,身体重心前移,左腿微屈独立支撑成左独立步,右腿屈膝前提,脚尖向下;左手下按在左胯旁,右勾手下落变掌向前上方挑起,掌心向左,指尖向上,高与眼平,右臂半屈成弧,肘关节与右膝相对;眼看右手。如图 5-136、图 5-137 所示。

图 5-136

图 5-137

2. 动作要点

(1) 注意动作的先后顺序,先屈收左小腿,右腿再屈膝下蹲。

(2) 由仆步转换成独立步时,做好前脚的外撇和后脚的内扣,独立步时身体重心要充分前移,右脚轻轻提起,不能出现右脚用力蹬地再起的现象。

（3）定势时，支撑腿微屈站稳，另一腿屈膝上提，小腿内收，脚尖下垂；头微上顶，上体正直挺拔。眼平视前方。

3. 易犯错误

仆步时动作不正确，出现塌腰突臀，上体过于前俯；独立步时重心不稳，出现后腿蹬地抬腿或拖泥带水的情况。

4. 纠正方法

加强对仆步正确动作要领的体会，仆步时脚尖内扣，膝部伸直，屈的腿全脚着地，臀部下沉，上体稍前倾；独立步时必须经过由仆步腿屈膝，靠后腿蹬地帮助完成到弓步的转变，并伴随重心充分前移，直至重心全部过渡到前面的支撑腿上，后腿才能干净利落地提起，加强腿部柔韧性和腿部力量练习，增强控制能力。

十七、右下式独立

1. 动作方法

右脚下落在左脚内侧前方，距左脚约一脚距离，脚尖着地；上体左转，以左脚前掌为轴向内扭转；左手成勾手向上提举于身体左侧，与肩同高，右手经头前划弧摆至左肩前，掌心向左；眼看勾手。如图5-138、图5-139所示。

左腿屈膝半蹲，右脚提起向右侧旁开一步，随重心下降右腿伸直，右脚全脚踏实；右掌在左胸前准备下落；眼看勾手。如图5-140所示。

左腿屈膝全蹲，上体右转成右仆步；右手经腹前沿右腿内侧向右穿出；眼看右掌。如图5-141所示。

重心移向右腿，右脚尖外撇，右腿屈膝前弓成右弓步；右手前穿向上挑起，左手在背后成勾手，勾尖向上；眼看右手。如图5-142所示。

上体微右转，身体重心继续前移，右腿独立支撑身体重量，左腿屈膝前提，脚尖向下；右手下按于右胯旁，左勾手变掌，经体侧向前挑起，掌心向右，指尖向上，高与眼平，左臂半屈成弧，肘关节与左膝相对；眼看左手。如图5-143、图5-144所示。

图5-138

图5-139

图5-140

图 5-141

图 5-142

图 5-143

图 5-144

2. 动作要点

左腿屈膝下蹲时右脚提起再伸出，不要不提脚就直接擦地伸出。

十八、左、右穿梭

1. 右穿梭动作方法

左脚向左前方下落，脚跟着地，脚尖外撇，上体左转重心前移，右脚收到左脚内侧；左手翻掌向下，右手翻掌向上，两手在左肋前成抱球姿势。如图 5-145～图 5-147 所示。

上体右转，右脚向右前方上步，右手向前上方划弧，左手向后下方划弧，两手交错；眼看右手。如图 5-148、图 5-149 所示。

上体继续右转，重心前移，右脚踏实成右弓步；右手翻转上举，架于右额前上方，掌心斜向上，左手经肋前推至体前与鼻同高；眼看左手。如图 5-150 所示。

图 5-145

图 5-146

图 5-147

图 5-148

图 5-149

图 5-150

2. 左穿梭动作方法

身体重心后移,右脚尖外撇,上体右转,右手下落于头前,左手稍向左划弧外展;眼看前方。如图 5-151、图 5-152 所示。

上体右转,两手在右肋前上下相抱,左脚收至右脚内侧,脚尖点地,眼看右手。如图 5-153 所示。

上体左转,左脚向左前方上步,脚跟着地;左手由下向前上方划弧,右手由上向后下方划弧,两手交错;眼看左手。如图 5-154、图 5-155 所示。

上体继续左转,身体重心前移,左脚踏实成左弓步;左手上举架于左额前上方,掌心向上,右手经肋前推至体前与鼻同高;眼看右手。如图 5-156 所示。

3. 动作要点

(1) 架推掌方向与中轴线成 30°角,弓步两脚宽约 30 厘米。

(2) 右穿梭过渡到左穿梭时,右脚尖不要外撇过大。

图 5-151

图 5-152

图 5-153

图 5-154

图 5-155

图 5-156

4. 易犯错误

动作方向不正确；架推掌太高。

5. 纠正方法

注意左右穿梭时，弓步应斜向前方约 30°角；架推掌时手置于右或左额前上方。

十九、海底针

1. 动作方法

右脚向前跟进半步距前脚约一脚长，然后重心后移右腿屈坐，上体右转，右手下落经体侧屈臂提抽至耳侧，掌心向左，指尖朝前，左手经体前向下划弧至腹前，掌心向下；眼看前方。如图 5-157、图 5-158 所示。

上体微左转向前俯身，左脚前移，脚前掌着地成左虚步；右手从耳侧向前下方插掌，掌心向左，指尖斜向前下方，左手经左膝前划弧搂过至大腿旁按掌；眼看右掌。如图 5-159 所示。

图 5-157

图 5-158

图 5-159

2. 动作要点

（1）上体舒展，前俯不超过 45°角。

（2）右手插掌时要向前下方直插，四指并拢，不要做成下劈或砍的动作。

3. 易犯错误

上体过分前俯左转，弯腰驼背，耸肩缩脖；右手插掌时做成下劈或砍的动作；虚步时前腿太直，身体重心太高，前倾突臀。

4. 纠正方法

定势时上体稍微前倾，保持头和躯干的端正，重心下沉，眼看前下方；插掌时，右手从耳侧直接向前下方插下去，右肩不要过分前顺；注意虚步时两腿的虚实比例，保持身体基本形态姿势，不挺髋挺腹；注意用腰部的转动来带动和协调全身的动作。

二十、闪通臂

1. 动作方法

图 5-160

图 5-161

图 5-162

上体稍右转,身体恢复正直,右手提至体前,掌心向左,指尖向前,左手屈臂收举于右腕内侧,左脚收至右脚内侧;眼看前方。如图 5-160 所示。

左脚向前迈出,重心前移成左弓步,左手向前平推,掌心向前,指尖与鼻尖相对齐,右手由体前上提,掌心外翻,右臂平屈于头侧上方,眼看左手。如图 5-161、图 5-162 所示。

2. 动作要点

(1) 弓步推掌左手、左腿上下相对,不能过分扭胯侧身做成侧弓步。

(2) 两手先上提再分开,左手经胸前向前推出,肘部保持微屈,不要伸直,右手上撑并微向后引拉。

二十一、转身搬拦捶

1. 动作方法

重心后移,右腿屈坐,左脚尖内扣,身体右转;两手向右侧摆动,右手摆至身体右侧,左手摆至头左侧,掌心均向外;眼看右手。如图 5-163 所示。

身体重心左移,左腿屈坐,右腿伸直,右脚跟提起向内转动;右手握拳下落经腹前向左划弧,停于左肋前,拳心向下,左手撑举于左额前;眼看前方。正反面示范如图 5-164、图 5-165 所示。

右脚提收至左脚踝关节内侧再向前垫步迈出,脚跟着地,脚尖外撇;右拳经胸上向前搬压,拳心向上,高与胸平,肘部微屈,左手经右前臂外侧下落,按于左胯旁;眼看右拳。正反面示范如图 5-166、图 5-167 所示。

上体右转,重心前移,左脚跟提起;右拳向右划弧至体侧,拳心向下,右臂半屈,左臂外旋,左手经左侧向体前划弧,掌心斜向上;眼看前方。如图 5-168、图 5-169 所示。

左脚向前上步,脚跟着地;左掌拦至体前,高与肩平,掌心向右,指尖斜向上,右拳翻转收在腰间,拳心朝上;眼看左掌。如图 5-170 所示。

上体左转,重心前移,左腿屈弓成左弓步,右腿自然蹬直;右拳从腰间向前打出,与胸同高,拳眼向上,左手微收附于右前臂内侧,掌心向右;眼看右拳。如图 5-171 所示。

图 5-163

图 5-164

图 5-165

图 5-166

图 5-167

图 5-168

图 5-169

图 5-170

图 5-171

2. 动作要点

（1）身体重心转换要清楚、平稳。

（2）垫步搬拳时注意右脚收至左脚内侧不点地直接迈出，脚尖外撇；垫步抬脚高度适宜，不要做成踩脚下落；搬拳时力点在拳背，右臂微屈。

（3）拦掌和收拳要协调同步，注意以腰带臂。

3. 易犯错误

转身搬拳时，重心起伏太大，右脚全脚落地，身体前移直接成弓步；拦掌时，左手外旋立掌做成左手心朝下、手指横向右的按掌；动作不连贯，重心起伏太大。

4. 纠正方法

转身搬拳时，重心保持平稳并侧重后坐于左脚，身体中正，右脚虚点，脚跟着地；拦掌时左手适当外旋带动左掌上立，力点在左掌指和掌心处；做动作时强调"意动身随""腰为主宰"，重心在动作变化过程中始终保持平稳。

二十二、如封似闭

1. 动作方法

左手翻转向上,经右前臂下向前穿出,右拳随之变掌,掌心向上,两掌在身体前交叉;眼看前方。如图 5-172 所示。

重心后移,右腿屈坐,左脚尖翘起;两臂屈收后引至胸前,掌心翻转斜向前下方;眼看前方。如图 5-173~图 5-175 所示。

重心前移,左腿屈弓成左弓步,两掌经胸前向前推出,高与肩平,与肩同宽,掌心向前,指尖向上;眼看前方。如图 5-176 所示。

图 5-172

图 5-173

图 5-174

图 5-175

图 5-176

2. 动作要点

后坐收掌时右腿屈膝缩髋,两臂屈收内旋,两手边收边翻转,不可卷肱扬手,两肘夹紧或抬肘耸肩。

二十三、十字手

1. 动作方法

上体右转，重心右移，左脚尖内扣；右手向右划弧摆动，两手心向外；眼看右手。如图 5-177 所示。

上体继续右转，右脚尖外撇，右腿屈膝侧弓，左腿自然伸直；右手右摆至身体右侧，两臂侧平举；眼看右手。如图 5-178 所示。

图 5-177

图 5-178

上体左转，重心左移落在左腿上，右脚脚尖内扣；两手准备向下划弧。如图 5-179 所示。

上体转向起势方向，右脚提起收拢半步，两手向下经腹前交叉上举，合抱于胸前；两腿慢慢直立，两脚平行成开立步；两臂撑圆，两腕交搭成十字形；眼看前方。如图 5-180 所示。

图 5-179

图 5-180

2. 动作要点

（1）两手从体侧划弧下落时不能弯腰低头。

（2）左脚内扣应转向起势方向，为收势作准备。

3. 易犯错误

转体成右侧弓步时右脚没有外摆造成右膝过分内扣紧髋；收脚合抱时突臀，身体前倾，直接收成并步站立。

4. 纠正方法

转体时左脚先内扣，重心右移，右脚以脚跟为轴外摆成右侧弓步；收脚合抱时，注意身体中正，臀部自然下坐，两眼平视；收脚合抱要求收右脚半步，保证双脚与肩同宽。

二十四、收势

1. 动作方法

两手臂内旋，两手翻转分开平举于体前，与肩同宽，掌心向下；眼看前方。如图 5-181、图 5-182 所示。

两臂徐徐下落于大腿外侧，左脚收回与右脚并拢，恢复成预备姿势。如图 5-183、图 5-184 所示。

图 5-181

图 5-182

图 5-183

图 5-184

2. 动作要点

（1）翻掌分手时，腕关节不要形成腕花。

（2）垂臂落手不能做成屈臂下按。

附：

SECTION I

1. Starting Form

(1) Stand upright with feet together. Slowly move left leg away from right leg so that legs are shoulder-width apart, arms hanging naturally at the outer side of legs. Eyes look straight ahead. Points for attention: Keep head and neck erect, with chin drawn slightly inward. Try not to protrude chest or draw in abdomen. Concentrate your attention on the exercise. (Fig 5-1, Fig 5-2)

(2) Raise arms slowly forward to shoulder level, with palms down. (Fig 5-3)

(3) Bend knees with torso remaining upright. At the same time, press palms down gently and drop elbows down toward knees. Eyes look straight ahead. (Fig 5-4, Fig 5-5)

Points for attention: Keep shoulders and elbows lowered, fingers naturally slightly curved and weight placed between legs. Bend knees and keep waist relaxed. Don't protrude buttocks. Arms should be lowered in coordination with the bending of knees.

2. Part the Wild Horse's Mane

(1) Turn torso slightly to the right and shift the weight to right leg. At the same time, raise right hand placing forearm horizontally in front of chest, palm down. Move left hand in a rightward-downward curve until it comes under right hand, palm up, as if you were holding a ball. Then bring left foot to the inner side of right foot, tiptoes touching ground. Eyes look at right hand. (Fig 5-6, Fig 5-7)

(2) Turn body to the left and move the left foot a step forward to the left before straightening right leg with heel on ground top form a left bow step. Meanwhile, separate hands and move them in two directions, with left hand going up to eye level, palm facing obliquely up and elbow slightly bent. Lower right hand down to the side of right hip, palm facing down and fingers pointing forward. Eyes look at left hand. (Fig 5-8～Fig 5-10)

(3) "Sit back" and shift weight to the right leg, with tiptoes of left foot slightly raised and turned outward. Then bend left leg and turn body to the left, with weight shifted to the left leg. Meanwhile, move left hand downward until it comes in front of the chest and right hand in a leftward-upward curve to make a hold-ball gesture, left hand on top. Then bring right foot to the inner side of left foot, tiptoes on ground. Eyes look at left hand. (Fig 5-11～Fig 5-13)

(4) Bend right leg at knee and move the foot a step forward to the right, and straighten left leg with heel on ground to form a right bow stance. Meanwhile, raise right hand to eye level with palm obliquely up and elbow slightly bent, and press left hand down to the side of left hip, palm facing downward and fingers pointing forward. Eyes look at right hand. (Fig 5-14～Fig 5-16)

(5) Repeat movements in (3), with "left" and "right" reversed. (Fig 5-17～Fig 5-19)

(6) Repeat movements in (4), with "left" and "right" reversed. (Fig 5-20～Fig 5-22)

Points for attention: Keep torso upright and chest relaxed. Make hand movements curved after you separate and move hands in different directions. Use the waist as an axis in body turns. The movements should be smooth when you take a bow stance and separate hands. When making a bow step, touch ground first with heel and then slowly with the whole foot. The knee of front leg should not be placed beyond the toes and rear leg should be straightened so that an angle of 45 degrees forms with ground. Keep a transverse distance of 10～30 centimeters between heels.

3. White Crane Spreads Its Wings

(1) Turn torso slightly to the left before moving left palm downward to the front of the chest and right hand in a leftward-upward curve to make a hold-ball gesture, left hand on top. (Fig 5-23)

(2) Move right foot half a step towards left foot and then sit back with weight shifted to the right leg. Move left foot a little bit forward, tiptoes on ground. At the same time, raise right hand to the front of right temple, palm turned inward, and move left hand down to the front of left hip, palm facing down. Eyes look straight ahead. (Fig 5-24, Fig 5-25)

Points for attention: Do not throw chest out. The movements should be rounded when you move arms upward or downward. Keep left knee slightly bent. Weight should be shifted in coordination with the movement of right hand.

SECTION II
4. Right and Left Brush Knee and Twist Step

(1) Move right hand downward before circling backward and upward to the outside of right shoulder, arm slightly bent, hand at ear level and palm facing up. Then move left hand in an upward-rightward-downward curve to the front of right part of chest, palm facing obliquely downward. Meanwhile, turn torso slightly to the left and then to the right. Eyes look at right hand. (Fig 5-26～Fig 5-28)

(2) Turn torso to the left and move left foot forward to the left to form a left bow step. Meanwhile, draw right hand past right ear before pushing it forward at nose level with palm facing forward. At the same time, left hand circles left knee until it comes beside left hip, palm facing down. Eyes look at fingers of right hand. (Fig 5-29, Fig 5-30)

(3) Sit back slowly with weight shifted to the right leg. Raise tiptoe of left foot and turn them a little bit outward. Then bend left leg slowly and turn body slightly to the left so that weight is shifted onto left leg. Move right foot forward to the inner side of left foot, tiptoes touching ground. Meanwhile, turn left palm up and move it forward and upward to shoulder level and move right hand in an upward-leftward-downward curve to the front of the left shoulder following the body turn, palm facing obliquely downward. Eyes look at left hand. (Fig 5-31～Fig 5-35)

(4) Repeat movements in (2), with "left" and "right" reversed. (Fig 5-36～Fig 5-40)

(5) Repeat movements in (3), with "left" and "right" reversed.

(6) Repeat movements in (2).

Points for attention: torso should be upright with waist relaxed, shoulders and elbows lowered when you push palm forward. Palm movements should be well-coordinated with those of waist and legs. Try to keep a transverse distance of 30 centimeters between heels in bow step.

5. Play the Lute

Move half a step forward. Then sit back and turn torso slightly to the right with weight transferred onto right leg. Lift left foot and move it a little forward, heel on ground and bend knee to form a left empty stance. Meanwhile, raise left hand in a leftward-downward-upward curve to nose-tip level, with elbow slightly bent, and move right hand back to the inner side of left elbow, palm facing leftward. Eyes look at forefinger of left hand. (Fig 5-41～Fig 5-43)

Points for attention: Keep body steady and natural and chest relaxed. The movement of left hand should be done in a leftward-upward-forward curve. Front part of the sole should be on ground first and then the whole foot when you move the right foot half a step forward. The shifting of weight and the raising of left hand should be well-coordinated.

6. Step Back and Whirl Arms

(1) Move the right hand with palm up in a downward-backward-upward curve past abdomen, arm slightly bent. Then turn left palm up and place tiptoes of left foot on ground. Eyes look to the right when you turn body to the right, and then at left hand when you turn it to the left. (Fig 5-44, Fig 5-45)

(2) Bend right elbow and push the right hand forward past right ear, palm facing forward. Withdraw the left hand to waist side before moving it in a backward-upward curve, palm up. With right palm turned up, lift left foot and move it a step backward, tiptoes on the ground. Then set the whole foot slowly on ground with weight shifted onto left leg to form a right empty stance. Eyes look at the left hand while turning the body and then at right hand. (Fig 5-46, Fig 5-47)

(3) Repeat movements in (2), with "left" and "right" reversed. (Fig 5-48～Fig 5-50)

(4) Repeat movements in (2). (Fig 5-51～Fig 5-53)

(5) Repeat movements in (2), with "left" and "right" reversed. (Fig 5-54～Fig 5-56)

Points for attention: Arms should not be too straight when you push them forward or move hands backward. Keep waist and hips relaxed when you push out hands. Movements of hands should be smooth and have the same tempo. Place tiptoes down first and then set the whole foot slowly on ground when you move left foot backward. At the same time, point front foot directly ahead. When you move the feet backward, tiptoes turn outward, so that they will not be placed on the same straight line. Eyes look to the left and right when you turn body, and then at the hand in front.

SECTION III

7. Grasp the Peacock's Tail on the Left

(1) Turn the body slowly to the right. Drop left hand naturally and move it in a curve past abdomen to the front of right ribs, palm up. Bend the right elbow, turn the palm down and draw it back to the front of the right chest. Keep both bands in a position as if to hold a ball, right hand on top. Meanwhile, turn tiptoes of right foot outward and move left foot to the inner side of right foot, tiptoes on the ground. Eyes look at the right hand. (Fig 5-57～Fig 5-59)

(2) Turn the body slightly to the left, move the left foot forward to the left and bend the left leg at knee to form a left bow step. At the same time, thrust out left arm to shoulder level as if to ward off a blow, palm backward. Drop the right hand slowly to the side of right hip, palm down. Eyes look at the left forearm. (Fig 5-60, Fig 5-61)

Points for attention: Arms should be rounded when you do the thrusting movement. Keep movements well-coordinated when you separate hands, turn waist and bend leg.

(3) Turning the body slightly to the left, stretch out left hand and turn the palm down. Turn right palm up and move it upward past the abdomen until it reaches below left wrist. Then, turn the torso slightly to the right, pull hands down in a rightward-backward curve past abdomen until right hand reaches shoulder level and left arm is bent in front of chest, with right palm up and left palm backward. At the same time, shift the body weight to the right leg. Eyes look at right hand. (Fig 5-62～Fig 5-64)

Points for attention: Do not lean forward or protrude buttocks when you pull down hands. The pulling movements should be done in a curve and with the turning of waist.

(4) Turning the torso slightly to the left, bend right arm and place the right hand inside left wrist, keeping a distance of five centimeters between them. Push both hands slowly forward, left palm backward and right palm forward, with left arm rounded. Simultaneously, shift the body weight to the left leg to form a left bow step. Eyes look at left wrist. (Fig 5-65, Fig 5-66)

Points for attention: Keep torso upright when you push hands forward. Hand movements should be well-coordinated with the turning of waist and bending of front leg.

(5) Extend right arm past left wrist to the front and right until it reaches the same level with left hand, palm down. Turn the left palm down. Move the hand apart to shoulder width. Sit back and shift weight to the right leg, tiptoes of left foot raised. Bend elbows and move hands back to the front of abdomen, palms facing forward. Eyes look straight ahead. (Fig 5-67, Fig 5-68)

(6) Continuing from the previous from, shift the body weight slowly to the left leg. At the same time, press palms forward up and bend left leg to form a left bow step. Eyes look straight ahead. (Fig 5-69, Fig 5-70)

Points for attention: The pressing movements should be done in a curve. Keep wrists at shoulder level and elbows bent.

8. Grasp the Peacock's Tail on the Right

(1) Sit back and turn torso to the right, with weight shifted to the right leg and tiptoes of left foot turned inward. Move right hand in a horizontal curve first to the right and then in a downward-leftward-upward curve past abdomen to the front of left chest, palm facing up. Bend the left arm in front of chest, left palm down, to join the right hand in a position as if to hold a ball. Meanwhile, shift weight to the left leg and move right foot to inside of left foot, tiptoes on the ground. Eyes look at left hand. (Fig 5-71～Fig 5-74)

(2) Repeat movements in 7 under (2), with "left" and "right" reversed. (Fig 5-75, Fig 5-76)

(3) Repeat movements in 7 under (3), with "left" and "right" reversed. (Fig 5-77, Fig 5-78)

(4) Repeat movements in 7 under (4), with "left" and "right" reversed. (Fig 5-79, Fig 5-80)

(5) Repeat movements in 7 under (5), with "left" and "right" reversed. (Fig 5-81～Fig 5-84)

(6) Repeat movements in 7 under (6), with "left" and "right" reversed. (Fig 5-85)

Points for attention: Same as those for 7.

SECTION IV

9. Single Whip

(1) Sit back and shift weight gradually to the left leg, tiptoes of right foot turned inward. At the same time, turn the body to the left and move both hands to the left, left hand on top, until left arm is extended on left side, palm leftward. Meanwhile, move right hand past abdomen to the front of left ribs, palm facing obliquely inward. Eyes look at left hand. (Fig 5-86, Fig 5-87)

(2) Shift weight gradually back to the right leg and move left foot close to the right foot, tiptoes on the ground. Meanwhile, move right hand upward to the right in a curve until right arm reaches shoulder level and change it into a hook on right side. Meanwhile, move left hand downward in a curve past abdomen until it comes in front of right shoulder, palm facing inward. Eyes look at left hand. (Fig 5-88, Fig 5-89)

(3) Turning body slightly to the left, move the left foot to the left side forward and straighten right leg to form a left bow step. Shift the body weight to the left leg while turning left palm slowly outward and pushing it forward with fingertips at eye level, palm forward, and elbow slightly bent. Eyes look at left hand. (Fig 5-90, Fig 5-91)

Points for attention: Keep torso upright, and relax the waist. Lower the right elbow. Left elbow should be placed above left knee and shoulders lowered. When you push left hand forward, the pushing movement should be done along with the turning of palm. Don't turn the palm over too fast. All the transitional movements must be well-coordinated.

10. Wave Hands Like Clouds

(1) Shift the body weight to the right leg, turn the body gradually to the right, left tiptoes inward. Then move left hand past abdomen to the right in a curve to the front of right shoulder, palm turned obliquely backward. At the same time, turn the right hand into palm, facing outward. Eyes look at right hand. (Fig 5-92, Fig 5-93)

(2) Shift the body weight slowly to the left leg, move left hand in a curve past face to the left, palm turned slowly leftward and move the right hand from the right blow and past the abdomen upward on the left in a curve to the front of right shoulder, palm obliquely backward. At the same time, move the right foot close to the left foot until they are parallel to each other and 10-20 centimeters apart. Eyes look at right hand. (Fig 5-94 ~Fig 5-98)

(3) Continue to move right hand to the right, and move the left hand past the abdomen in a curve to the right upward to the front of right shoulder, palm obliquely backward. At the same time, turn the right palm over to the right and move the left foot a step to the left. Eyes look at left hand. (Fig 5-99~Fig 5-101)

(4) Repeat movements in (2). (Fig 5-102~Fig 5-104)

(5) Repeat movements in (3). (Fig 5-105~Fig 5-106)

Points for attention: Body turn should be done with the waist as an axis. Keep waist and hips relaxed. Try to avoid rising or falling abruptly. Arm movements should be natural, circular and coordinated with the turning of waist. Speed should be slow and even. Keep your balance when you do movements with the lower limbs. Eyes should follow the movements of both hands.

11. Single Whip

(1) Continue to move right hand to the right until it is turned into a hook on right side. At the same time, move left hand in a rightward-upward curve past abdomen to the front of right shoulder with palm turned inward. Shift the body weight to the right leg, tiptoes of left foot on the ground. Eyes look at left hand. (Fig 5-107～Fig 5-109)

(2) Turn the body slightly to the left, move the left foot a step to the left and straighten right leg to form a left bow step. While the body weight is shifted to the left leg, turn the left hand over and push it forward. Eyes look at left hand. (Fig 5-110, Fig 5-111)

Points for attention: Same as those for 9.

SECTION Ⅴ

12. Pat Horse from on High

(1) Move the right foot half a step forward and shift the body weight to the right leg. Then, change the right hook hand into a palm and turn both palms upward, both elbows slightly bent. Meanwhile, turn body slightly to the right and raise left heel gradually to form a left empty stance. Eyes look at left hand. (Fig 5-112, Fig 5-113)

(2) Turn the body slightly to the left, push right palm forward past right ear with fingertips at eye level, and withdraw the left hand to the side of left hip, palm up. At the same time, move the left foot slightly forward, tiptoes on the ground. Eyes look at right hand. (Fig 5-114)

Points for attention: Keep torso naturally upright with shoulders lowered and right elbow slightly downward.

13. Kick with Right Heel

(1) Turn the left palm upward and move it forward until it crosses right hand at wrist. Then separate hands and move them in a downward curve with palms turned obliquely downward. At the same time, raise left foot and move it forward to the left to form a left bow step, tiptoes slightly outward. Eyes look straight ahead. (Fig 5-115～Fig 5-117)

(2) Move hands in a curve up from the sides of the body and cross them in front of chest, with right hand outside and both palms turned inward. At the same time, move the right foot to the inner side of left foot, tiptoes on the ground. Eyes look forward to the right. (Fig 5-118)

(3) Separate hands and extend both arms sideways to shoulder level, elbows slightly bent and palms turned outward. At the same time, lift right leg and kick with right heel slowly forward to the right. Eyes look at right hand. (Figs 5-119, Fig 5-120)

Points for attention: Keep the body stable. Keep wrists at shoulder level when the hands are moved apart. Bent the left leg slightly, and right tiptoes backward when kicking. The moving of hands and the kicking of right foot should be well-coordinated. Keep the right arm and right leg on a vertical line when kicking.

14. Strike Opponent's Ears with Both Fists

(1) Withdraw the right leg, bend the knee and raise it horizontally. Move left hand from behind, upward and forward, and drop it in front of the chest, palms turned inward. Then move hands downward in a curve and bring them to each side of right knee with palms up. (Fig 5-121)

(2) Set right foot on ground to the right and shift the body weight gradually to the right leg to form a right bow step. At the same time, lower the hands, change them into fists slowly, and move them upward from both sides and curve them to the front of the face and forward like pliers, fist to fist with a distance of 10-20 centimeters apart. Eyes look at right fist. (Fig 5-122, Fig 5-123)

Points for attention: Keep head and neck erect, waist and hips relaxed and hands loosely clenched. Shoulders and elbows should be lowered and arms rounded.

15. Turn and Kick with Left Heel

(1) Shift the body weight to the left leg and turn body to the left with right tiptoes inward (about 90 degrees). At the same time, turn both fists into palms and move them in an upward-downward curve from above to both sides, and raise them horizontally. Eyes look at the left hand. (Fig 5-124, Fig 5-125)

(2) Shift the body weight to the right leg and bring left foot to the inner side of right foot, tiptoes on the ground. At the same time, move both hands in an outward-upward-inward curve until they cross at wrist in front of chest, with left hand in front and palms facing inward. Eyes look to the left. (Fig 5-126, Fig 5-127)

(3) Separate hands and extend arms to each side at shoulder level, elbows slightly bent and palms facing outward. At the same time, lift left leg and kick forward with left foot slowly to the left. Eyes look at left hand. (Fig 5-128, Fig 5-129)

Points for attention: All same as those for 13 except that "right" and "left" are reversed.

SECTION Ⅵ

16. Push Down and Stand on Left Leg

(1) Withdraw the left leg and lift it to thigh level. Change right hand into a hook, turn up left palm and move it in an upward-rightward-downward curve to the front of right shoulder. Eyes look at right hand. (Fig 5-130~Fig 5-132)

(2) Squat down slowly on right leg and stretch left leg to the left for a left crouch step. Then move left hand down and to the left along the inner side of left leg. Eyes look at left hand. (Fig 5-133, Fig 5-134)

Points for attention: When you squat down, try to avoid leaning too much forward and straighten left leg. The tiptoes of the left foot should be turned slightly inward and in line with right heel. The soles of both feet should be placed on the ground.

(3) With tiptoes of the left foot turned slightly outward and those of right foot inward, bend left leg and straighten right leg. Turn torso slightly to the left with left heel as an axis before rising up to the front. At the same time, continue to move left arm forward, palm facing to the right. Eyes look at left hand. (Fig 5-135)

(4) Lift right leg slowly and bend it at knee to stand on the left leg. At the same time, move right hand downward and turn it into palm. Swing it to the front past outside of right leg, arm bent above right knee and palm facing left. Meanwhile, drop the left hand to the si8de of left hip, palm downward. Eyes look at right hand. (Fig 5-136, Fig 5-137)

Points for attention: Keep torso upright, with the supporting leg slightly bent and tiptoes of the raising leg pointing downward naturally.

17. Push Down and Stand on Right Leg

(1) Plant the right foot in front of left foot, tiptoes on the ground. Then turn the body to the left with the ball of left foot as an axis. At the same time, raise left hand sideways to shoulder level and change it into a hook. Move the right hand in a leftward curve to the front of left shoulder, fingers pointing up. Eyes look at left hand. (Fig 5-138, Fig 5-139)

(2) Repeat movements in 16 under (2), with "left" and "right" reversed. (Fig 5-140, Fig 5-141)

(3) Repeat movements in 16 under (3), with "left" and "right" reversed. (Fig 5-142)

(4) Repeat movements in 16 under (4), with "left" and "right" reversed. (Fig 5-143, Fig 5-144)

Points for attention: Raise the right tiptoes a bit after they touch the ground, then crouch. Other points are the same as those for 16 except that "left" and "right" are reversed.

SECTION VII

18. Shuttle Back and Forth

(1) Turn the body slightly to the left and land the left foot forward, tiptoes outward and right heel slightly raised to form a half "sitting position with legs crossed." At the same time, place both hands in front of left part of the chest as if to hold a ball, left hand on top. Then bring right foot to the inner side of left foot, tiptoes on the ground. Eyes look at left forearm. (Fig 5-145~Fig 5-147)

(2) Move the right foot forward to the right to form a right bow step. At the same time, raise right hand up past face to the front of right forehead, palm turned obliquely upward. Move the left hand first down on the left side and then past the front of the body and push it forward to the height of the nose tip, palm forward. Eyes look at left hand. (Fig 5-148～Fig 5-150)

(3) Shift weight slightly backward as you turn slightly to the right. Turn tiptoes of right foot a little bit outward, shifting weight back onto right leg and bringing left foot to the inner side of right foot, tiptoes on the ground. At the same time, place hand sin front of right part of the chest as if to hold a ball, right hand on top. Eyes look at right forearm. (Fig 5-151～Fig 5-153)

(4) Repeat movements in (2), with "left" and "right" reversed. (Fig 5-154～Fig 5-156)

Points for attention: Try to avoid leaning forward when you push left hand and lifting shoulders when you raise right hand. The pushing and raising movements should be well-coordinated with the forming of right bow step. There should be a transverse distance of about 30 centimeters between heels in bow step.

19. Needle at the Sea Bottom

Move the right foot half a step forward and left foot a little bit forward with tiptoes on the ground to form a left empty stance. At the same time, turn the body slightly to the right, move the right hand in a downward-backward-upward curve past the front of the body and thrust it forward down past right ear, fingertips downward, while move the left hand in a forward-downward curve to the side of left hip, palm down. Eyes look ahead. (Fig 5-157～Fig 5-159)

Points for attention: Turn body first to the right and then to the left. Try to avoid leaning too far forward and keep head erect and buttocks drawn in. Left leg should be bent slightly.

20. Flash Arms

Turn the body slightly to the right and move left foot forward to form a left bow step. At the same time, raise right hand, turn palm upward, bend the arm, raise it up and rest it above in front of the right forehead, with thumb downward. Move left hand upward and push it forward at nose-tip level. Eyes look at left hand. (Fig 5-160～Fig 5-162)

Points for attention: Keep the torso naturally upright and waist and hips relaxed. Try to avoid straightening the arm when you push left palm forward. Back muscles should be stretched. The pushing movement and the forming of bow step should be well-coordinated.

SECTION VIII

21. Turn Body and Punch

(1) Sit back and shift the body weight to the right leg, tiptoes of left foot turned inward. Then turn the body to the right and shift the body weight again to the left leg. At the same time, with the turning of the body, move the right hand in a rightward-downward curve past abdomen to the side of left ribs, hand turned into fist and palm facing downward. Raise the left palm upward to the front of forehead, palm obliquely upward. Eyes look straight ahead. (Fig 5-163～Fig 5-165)

(2) Continue to turn the body to the right and move right first past the chest upward, forward and downward for a punch, palm inward. Drop the left hand to the side of left hip. At the same time, withdraw the right foot and then move it forward again, tiptoes outward. Eyes look at right fist. (Fig 5-166, Fig 5-167)

(3) Shift the body weight to the right leg and move left foot a step forward. Meanwhile, raise the left hand up and move it forward for a parry, palm forward. At the same time, withdraw the right hand by the right hip, eye of fist up. Eyes look at left hand. (Fig 5-168～Fig 5-170)

(4) Bend left leg to form a left bow step. At the same time, thrust right fist forward at chest level for a punch, eye of fist up. Grab the inner side of the right forearm with the left palm. Eyes look at right fist. (Fig 5-171)

Points for attention: Do not clench right fist tightly. When withdrawing the right fist to the side of right hip, keep forearm rotating, with fist turned down and up again. When thrusting right fist forward, extend the right shoulder a little bit forward. Keep shoulders and elbows lowered and bend the right arm slightly.

22. Close Up

(1) Move left hand forward from under right wrist, turning fist into palm. Turn palms upward and pull them back slowly. Meanwhile, sit back with tiptoes of left foot raised and shift the body weight to the right leg. Eyes look straight ahead. (Fig 5-172～Fig 5-174)

(2) Turn palms downward in front of chest, move both hands back to the front of abdomen and push them forward with wrists at shoulder level and palms facing forward. Meanwhile, bend left leg to form a left bow step. Eyes look straight ahead. (Fig 5-175, Fig 5-176)

Points for attention: Do not lean backward or protrude buttocks when sitting back. When withdrawing the arms, do not pull them straight to the back, keep shoulders relaxed and elbows turned a little bit outward. The distance of hands should be no greater than shoulder-width.

23. Cross Hands

(1) Shift the body weight to the right leg and turn the body to the right, tiptoes of left foot turned inward. With the body turning, move the right hand sideways in a horizontal curve with elbows lowered. At the same time, turn tiptoes of the right foot slightly outward with body turn to forma right bow step. Eyes look at right hand. (Fig 5-177, Fig 5-178)

(2) Shift the body weight slowly to the left leg, move right foot to the side of left foot, the distance between the feet being shoulder width. At the same time, move hands down in a downward-upward curve past abdomen until they cross at wrists in front of the chest, right hand in front and palms inward. Eyes look straight ahead. (Fig 5-179, Fig 5-180)

Points for attention: Try to avoid leaning the body forward when the hands are separated and crossed. Keep body and head erect and chin tucked slightly inward when standing. Keep arms rounded and comfortable with shoulders and elbows lowered.

24. Finishing Form

Turn palms downward and drop hands gradually to both sides of the body. Stand naturally. Eyes look straight ahead. (Fig 5-181～Fig 5-184)

Points for attention: Keep whole body relaxed and draw a deep breath when the hands are separated and dropped. Be sure to keep exhalation protracted for a little while. Then move the left foot close to right foot when your breath becomes even. Take a walk for a full rest.

Note

The paths of the movements are indicated by arrows, with solid lines for the right hand and foot, but dotted lines for the left hand and foot.

第六章　简化太极拳健身指导

虽然太极拳是柔和的全身运动,但利用太极拳进行健身的时候,仍然需要注意锻炼手段和方法,严格遵循太极拳练习的规范标准,科学合理地进行太极拳练习活动。本章重点对简化太极拳的正确锻炼方法和技术指导进行介绍,并对练习太极拳时应注意的事项及常见损伤与预防等方面的内容做了详细说明。为了避免不必要的损伤,同时极大地发挥太极拳的健身效果,本章内容亟待太极拳习练者给予重视。

第一节　锻炼方法和技术指导

太极拳是柔和的全身运动,着重思想即意念的训练,由大脑有意识地指挥身体活动。练习时要求全身放松,不得有僵滞之处,才能使全身气血流畅,身心愉悦,缓解大脑疲劳,提高工作效率。对于某些体弱及患病的人,有帮助恢复体力,促进疾病痊愈的功能。现在全民健身的新概念是倡导进行有氧运动[①],而太极拳则是有氧运动典型代表,所以,我们在利用太极拳进行健身的时候,其锻炼手段和方法的选择更丰富、灵活、多样,不拘形式。

一、原地动作锻炼法

(1) 太极拳桩功练习:如无极桩、虚实桩、开合桩、太极桩和起落桩,任选一到两种方法进行练习,练习时长应在身体自然舒适,心静,呼吸自然,腿部无明显疲劳感的前提下,坚持20分钟左右为宜。

(2) 在站桩的基础上,原地上肢动作组合练习:如在原地抱球左右野马分鬃、原地左右白鹤亮翅、原地左右搂膝拗步、原地左右云手、原地左右倒卷肱、原地左右揽雀尾、原地左右穿梭等动作的单一上肢动作。在自己熟悉的动作中选几式重复的连贯练习。在练习过程中注意呼吸自如,眼随手走,以腰为轴,重心平稳,身体中正,并保持练习时间在20分钟左右。

(3) 原地下肢步法练习:如原地左右弓步转换、原地左右提膝、原地左右蹬脚的重复连贯练习。在练习过程中注意呼吸自然,身体中正,重心平稳,无明显起伏和身体的摇晃,并保持练习时间在20分钟左右。

(4) 原地完整单个动作的重复练习:如在原地抱球左右野马分鬃、原地左右白鹤亮翅、

---

① 有氧运动是指机体长时间进行运动(耐力运动),使得心(血液循环系统)、肺(呼吸系统)得到充分的有效刺激,提高心、肺功能。从而让全身各组织、器官得到良好的氧气和营养供应,维持最佳的功能状况。

原地左右搂膝拗步、原地左右云手、原地左右倒卷肱、原地左右揽雀尾、原地左右穿梭、原地左右独立式、原地左右蹬脚等。在自己熟悉并掌握情况较好的动作中选出几式连贯重复练习，并保证动作要领正确，时长在 20 分钟左右。

二、 行进动作锻炼法

（1）行进间下肢步法练习：如进步、后退步、侧行步重复连贯的练习。进步和侧行步时双手背于后腰处，后退步时双手重叠放于丹田处。保证呼吸自然，身体重心平稳，身体中正不摇晃，时长 20 分钟左右。

（2）行进间单个完整动作或动作小组，反复数遍的练习：不拘于套路中对每式动作练习次数的限制，可据场地情况无限反复连贯地练习某一式或几式动作数次，以达到一定的运动量及健身的目的。如单一地行进间野马分鬃数次，或是行进间野马分鬃，行进间搂膝拗步，行进间倒卷肱，行进间左右云手、左右下势独立、左右穿梭等动作，任选其中自己掌握的较为熟练的几式动作串编成动作小组合，保证动作正确，流畅，时长 20 分钟左右。

（3）二十四式太极拳分动作组合练习：按照二十四式太极拳的套路顺序，每四个动作分为一组来进行分组合后的反复练习。可以一直练习某四个动作的一个组合，也可以按顺序把二十四式太极拳分为六个小组动作来依次练习，组合与组合动作间可以适当地休息。

（4）二十四式太极拳完整套路的练习：这也是人们最常用的练习方法和误认为太极拳作为健身手段只能是这样成套的方法。练习二十四式太极拳全套动作，根据练习者的状态不同，水平高低的不同可用时 3~6 分钟不等，要达到健身的效果和目的，一般要反复练习全套动作 2~3 遍，完成一套动作的练习后注意时到休息。练习时间保持在 20 分钟，不宜过度练习导致身体疲劳而影响工作和休息。

（5）可配上自己喜爱的柔和悠扬的音乐来进行太极拳的练习：达到健身的同时也健心和陶冶情操的目的，为自己的练习增添情趣，减少枯燥，并帮助自己更好地融入太极拳练习的意境中，保持心情愉悦。

（6）也可综合上述部分锻炼方法进行练习：可按锻炼方法手段介绍的先后顺序选择进行，原则要求动作由简到繁，由易到难，先分解动作后完整动作，运动量由小到大。如先站几分钟桩功后再进行下肢步法的练习，再进行原地上肢动作练习，再进行完整动作的练习或是进入整套练习。总之遵循循序渐进，逐步深入的方法。这样既丰富了练习的内容，减少了单一重复的枯燥性，又在练习的同时有序地增强和提高动作质量。

太极拳锻炼的方法很多，很难说哪一种方法就一定合适自己。也许通过长时间的太极拳的练习和领悟，会发现更为科学合理并适合自己练习的锻炼方法和手段。但只有坚持才是真理，哪怕只是反复练习一式或几式动作，否则三天打鱼两天晒网，再好的练习方法也不能达到满意的效果。练习者中存在一种对太极拳作为健身手段和方法的较片面的理解和做法，即是：太极拳练习只是一味追求套路的完整性或是套路的多样性，或是必须按太极拳的套路顺序来练习，或是必须在音乐的伴奏下才能够进行练习。实质上，太极拳练习者也可从中截取一些自己熟悉和喜爱的动作，用拆招的上、下肢分解练习法和完整动作左右式的反复练习法。只要把握好练习的原则和要领，以及练习时间和强度，不按套路顺序同样可以达到健身的功效。

第二节　太极拳练习时的注意事项及常见损伤与预防

一、练习太极拳时应注意的事项

（1）练拳前应作适当的放松调整，做到心平气和、思想集中。结束练习后，不可立即停下，应做适当地调息运动，如一呼一吸迈一步的缓慢散步呼吸方法，注意意守丹田。也可原地进一步伸展身体各部位、牵拉运动等，精神不可散乱，让心律逐渐平复到接近练拳前的安静状态并保持精神愉快、心情舒畅。

（2）练拳时姿势一定要正确，动作要合乎规范，否则错误动作定势后较难纠正甚至还会给身体造成不良的影响。坚持练习不间断，才能获得增强体质的良好效果。

（3）练拳时要选择适宜的环境，尽量在阳光充足、空气清新、地面平坦、环境幽静的空地上练习，注意保暖。

（4）每天清晨或傍晚练拳较好，早晨空气清新，环境安静，锻炼时可充分调动人体各器官的功能，为一天的工作和学习做好身心准备；傍晚练拳则可消除疲劳，稍平气息，帮助睡眠提高睡眠质量。工间休息或课间休息时间练拳则可提神醒脑，减缓大脑疲劳（适合脑力劳动的人群）。但要提醒注意的是，晨练要避雾：雾是空气中水汽的凝结物，其中含有较多的酸、碱、胺、酚、二氧化硫、硫化氢、尘埃和病原微生物等有害物质。锻炼时吸入过多的雾气，可损害呼吸道和肺泡，引起咽炎、支气管炎和肺炎等疾病。

（5）练拳时运动量应适中。练拳时长 20～30 分钟为宜（不包括热身运动和结束放松部分）。体弱者可据自己的身体情况适当减小运动量，缩短运动时间或降低练习密度，延长休息时间。

（6）饥饿或饱食后不易练拳。一般饭后 30 分钟再练拳；练拳后不易立即吃饭或大量饮水，最好间隔 20 分钟后再进行。

（7）练拳时衣着要宽松舒适，尤其是鞋子要鞋底、鞋面、脚踝处松软，保证脚各部位的灵活性及血流的通畅。

（8）习练太极拳过程中，要避免常见的技术错误而导致的身体发抖和膝关节疼痛。

二、练习太极拳时身体某些部位或全身发抖的原因与预防

1. 出现发抖的原因

（1）由于姿势要领掌握不准，过分追求太极拳的外形和身体的外部表现，从而造成而身体、意念紧张，想松不能松。追求动作的过分缓慢，呼吸不能自然舒畅，或是出现劳累，从而导致技术性错误而身体发抖。

（2）身体不适，阻塞经络的气血运行，从而气血大量集聚于此，强行通过又不能，就造成身体病理性发抖现象。

2. 改进办法

（1）是因为错误的意念和错误的动作造成的发抖现象，应加强多动作技术要领的体会，

练拳前一定做到心静体松,抛开一切顾虑和杂念,全神贯注于动作的练习中,做到眼随手走,意识引导动作,提高动作熟练性,注意动作的规范、流畅,呼吸的自然平和和身体的安舒状态,不过分追求自己完不成的动作要领,如追求重心过分低的姿势和过分慢的速度。掌握好循序渐进的原则,科学性合理安排运动量。也可在练习中配以柔和轻灵的音乐帮助自己的意念放松,进入良好的太极拳练习意境和状态中,保证动作在流畅的基础上缓慢,而不是越慢越好。如此便能逐渐克服发抖现象。

(2) 发抖的存在促使气血冲过阻塞,活络筋血,长此下去,能起到调节身体精血、畅通经络、修复身体病灶、健康身体的作用。随着练习者长期不懈地坚持,伴随身体的发抖现象也会逐渐消除。因此,要正确区分发抖原因。出现发抖,待练习结束后,如果身体轻松、舒畅、呼吸自然、则为正常的发抖现象;若出现劳累,呼吸急促,较长时间不能平复到安静状态或身体动作僵硬发抖,则应注意减小运动量。

三、练习太极拳时出现膝关节疼痛的原因和预防

1. 练习太极拳时出现膝关节疼痛的原因

(1) 运动量过大,劳累。太极拳练习过程中,膝关节始终处于半蹲位和静力性支撑姿势。与日常生活不同,此时,膝关节的负重很大,如果长时间过量、单一地进行锻炼,就容易导致膝关节疼痛,感觉膝软无力。初期疼痛症状不是很明显,只是感觉膝部酸痛,只要练拳时稍加注意,略微提高练拳姿势,疼痛感便消失。但随着练习时间的加长、练习天数的增多,疼痛会明显加重,不仅练拳时疼痛,即使抬高重心,甚至上下楼梯时也痛,休息后疼痛可减轻。但若恢复较大运动量的锻炼,症状就会重新出现并且加重。

(2) 弓步转换时要领不正确,膝关节时常处于伸直状态。以正弓步举例:杨式太极拳中虚、实腿是相对于支撑人体重量的多少而定的。正弓步时前腿弓、后腿蹬,前脚承受体重约六成,后脚承受体重约四成。则前腿为实腿,后腿为虚腿,前腿碾转的基本要领是在全身放松的基础上,脚尖翘,以脚跟为轴碾转(不减少该脚的承重),碾转中必须使脚尖、膝尖、手尖、鼻尖及眼神等同时转,膝部自然微曲,身法仍保持中正。如果在碾转过程中身体用力不顺,或碾转中不自然屈膝,重心不能及时跟进并分担一部分身体重量给大腿肌肉,腰无法保持中正,会使膝关节的两侧受到挤压,韧带过分牵拉和上下关节面上下受到过重的挤压,导致膝关节疼痛。由于不能很好地掌握弓步碾转过程中的身体要领,常在碾转中膝关节用力里扣或外旋来带领脚尖的转动。或者是脚尖先转动,膝关节紧跟着转动,而身子迟随,身重压迫膝关节的侧面,使膝关节内侧肌、韧带产生慢性损伤,这样的错误动作只要连续出现在几天的练习中膝关节就会疼痛难受,越练越痛,严重时甚至会导致关节积水影响生活,让习拳者望而生畏,不再打拳。

(3) 弓步时屈膝过度。屈膝腿的膝尖与脚尖方向不一,膝关节过分内扣或外展。膝关节所受的分力将向膝侧面挤压,时间一长会导致韧带过累而膝部疼痛;屈膝腿前弓过度。常见的膝尖超过脚尖,尤其是两脚前后的跨度小,胯一沉,前腿屈膝膝尖很易超过脚尖。这时膝关节所受的身体重力过大,股骨关节面过于前弓紧压膝盖之髌骨,时间一长髌骨将劳损而疼痛。

2. 改进办法

(1) 上诉现象若不引起重视,随着膝关节疲劳损伤的加重极易形成膝关节髌骨软骨病。

特别需要引起我们注意的是：髌骨的再生能力很低，如果一旦髌骨损伤，就很难修复。适当减小运动量，保证每天的练习时间在20～30分钟即可。重心不宜过低，膝屈130°左右为适宜高度。当膝关节酸痛感刚出现时应引起重视，及时查明酸痛的原因，如是练习时间过长引起，应及早减小运动量和抬高重心，缓解膝部疲劳，以防止疼痛加剧和膝关节受伤。大约一个月左右酸痛感会消失。但当经过休息和抬高重心、减量练习，仍不能缓解和消除膝关节疼痛时，应立即停止练习，去专业医院治疗。

（2）反复体会弓步的要领，可配合原地或行进间的单独弓步练习来纠正错误的弓步动作。着重体会进步或退步时腰的转动和身体各部位的协调用力与配合，保证身体不出现拧劲，身体中正不前倾。转动过程中注意膝关节适中的自然曲。避免出现膝关节过直身体重心全压在膝关节上的现象。

（3）加强腿部柔韧性和力量练习，加强关节灵活性。以保证腿部有充足的力量满足重心持久较低姿势和承受身体重量的需要，伸屈拧转自如。同时加大弓步步幅，保持好弓步时屈膝130°左右为适宜高度，不过分追求完不成的低姿势（始终保持弓步时前屈的大腿与地面平），膝关节与脚尖一线，不得超过脚尖。膝关节中正不过分内扣和外摆。欲速则不达，循序渐进，慢慢提高。只有身体素质提高了，太极拳技术才能更上一个台阶，同时才能减少损伤的发生。

（4）重视准备活动和练后放松。

第三节　太极拳训练时的易犯错误及纠正方法

太极拳的训练过程分为三个阶段，即基础训练阶段，专项提高阶段，强化套路训练阶段。

一、基础训练阶段，即盘架（练架）阶段

从基本动作乃至套路动作必须按照动作要领一招一式反复练习，建立规范、正确的动作动力定型。此阶段容易出现的错误如下。

1. 身法不正、低头猫腰

太极拳要求立身中正、提顶吊裆、含胸拔背、空胸实腹。但初学者由于理解与实际水平相去甚远，同时身体肌肉感觉及控制力较差，尤其是背部的竖脊肌、腰方肌、臀大肌等肌肉力量尚小，往往会出现低头猫腰、驼背等错误现象。

纠正方法：

（1）用器械辅助练习，如负重弓身、负重转腰等，增强腰肌力量；

（2）两手扶丹田的升降练习，可想象头顶着一碗水进行练习，注意要空胸实腹、意守丹田、逆式呼吸，动作要缓慢、均匀；

（3）两手扶丹田，命门后撑，两肘稍外张，想象两肩与两髋关节构成的圆柱体做左右旋转练习。

2. 步型、手型、身法、步法不清

太极拳的手型各式之间存在差异，其身法、步型、步法与外家拳也不同，初学者往往将它

们混淆,尤其是弓步后蹬脚不能完全蹬直,独立动作的支撑脚不能站直,上肢冲拳或推掌时肘关节不能伸直。

纠正方法:

(1) 掌握太极拳独特的身法、手型手法、步型步法的概念,定式练习;

(2) 不断地进行对比练习(或对镜练习),2~3人一组,相互纠正。

3. 立身不稳、虚实不清

太极拳的脚步移动、前进、后退与外家拳有所不同。凡是向前迈步,要求支撑腿下沉坐稳,运动腿脚后跟先着地,然后是脚掌、脚趾,再过渡到全脚掌着地,后退则完全相反。虚实转换要分清。"迈步如猫行""如履薄冰"是太极拳脚步移动生动、形象的描述。太极拳要求重心平稳,动作轻灵沉稳,两膝运动如"揉面"一样圆活。但是,初学者往往会出现立身不稳、动作虚实不清,重心高低起伏,上、下动作不一致等错误。主要原因是腿部力量较差,对太极拳独特的运动方式把握不准,重心虚实转换不明。

纠正方法:

(1) 双手扶丹田前进、后退的移动练习、单腿独立平衡动作的持久性练习;

(2) 加强腿部肌肉力量锻炼,如负重半蹲、负重前进、后退的移动练习,升降开合桩练习;

(3) "推腿练习":两人一组,正面弓步相对,两手扶丹田或两手背叠于命门处,两人前腿踝关节内侧靠拢,以小腿膝关节为接触点,重心前后移动,做弓步等虚步的转换练习,接触点做顺时针或逆时针的圆弧运动;

(4) 减小运动量的练习,套路练习时适当调高架子,减小运动幅度;

(5) 加强太极拳意识的培养,掌握太极拳独特的思维方式。

二、专项提高阶段

此阶段要打破传统的训练程序法"先强调套路训练,化刚为柔,由柔至刚,由着熟而渐悟懂劲。"重点是先加强功力训练和用太极意识的身体素质练习,提高自身的"质量"(即运动能力),通过各种推手、"喂劲"及专项素质训练方法,使中枢神经系统与运动系统达成高度协调,在推手训练中培养听劲、化劲、粘劲、掤劲等劲法,培养自身的感知能力、条件反射能力和快速反击能力。此阶段容易出现的错误有:推手时有"蛮力""拙力",怕输而产生"顶牛"现象;自身的感知能力、条件反射能力和快速反击能力较差,太极战术意识较差等。

纠正方法:

(1) 两人一组在"不丢不顶""轻灵圆活"状态下定步、活步推手;

(2) 两人一组的"喂"劲练习,不同对手练习、不同体重级别之间的散推练习;

(3) 利用器械辅助练习:"抱球转球"练习、拉橡皮筋、抖大杆练习。

三、强化套路训练阶段

在掌握各种推手技术、获得一定劲力的基础上,强调柔化训练,强调心、意、气内三合和外三合,着重提高套路的正确性、规范性,培养机体的高度协调能力,掌握太极拳演练技巧和水平。此阶段容易出现的错误有:呼吸与动作开合不协调,动作还比较僵硬不规范、节奏不明显、发劲力点不准、动作不到位、攻防意识不强、风格不够突出等。

纠正方法：

（1）加强太极拳的拳理学习，加强太极拳运动的美学研究，严格按照太极拳的演练标准进行练习；

（2）观看高水平队员的比赛录像，了解名人名家的演练风格、特色，取长补短，加深动作印象，邀请太极拳名家或高水平的教练做指导，进行综合的技术诊断；

（3）通过动作单练、反复地发劲练习，悉心体会动作的虚实、轻重、劲力走向、手法腿法的攻防含义；

（4）加强动作开合与呼吸配合的开合桩练习。

第四节　技术发展不同阶段的要求

一、技术发展的三个阶段

太极拳习练者技术的提高及动作掌握情况一般分为基础、提高、自如三个阶段。每个技术阶段对习练者的技术要领要求不同。

（1）基础阶段的技术训练要领是：体松心静，身体中正，安舒自然，动作、技法规范准确，动作轻灵平稳、舒展柔和，眼随手走，神态自然。这个时期练习时要注意：动作要慢，力量要轻，动作造型和运动路线要圆。

（2）提高阶段的技术要领是：动作上下相随、连贯圆活、虚实分明、呼吸自然。这个时期练习时要注意：动作衔接要连贯，动作力量要轻柔，身体各部位的配合要完整。

（3）自如阶段训练的技术要领是：以意导体、分清虚实、以气运身、气力相合、神韵充盈、从容自如。追求意、气、形的完美结合，内外合一，形神兼备。这个时期要注意的是：要意识领导动作，动作和呼吸配合要顺畅，动作做到刚柔相济。

习练者应纠正注重表面形式的错误观念，尽量追求"用意不用力"的自如最高境界。也有练太极拳讲究一不用气，用气则滞；二不用力，用力则断；三不用法，用法则尽一说。这里所说的"气"是指"怒气"，"力"是指拙力和硬力，"法"则指主观的、不合规矩的陋习和方法。习练者在太极拳练习中，应合理运气，用力和保持身形、动作的规范，遵守太极拳的练习法则，这样才能更好地提高太极拳技术水平。

二、技术提升的条件

欲求达到高深的地步，必须有以下几种精神才能成功。

（1）有恒心：练习太极拳需有长性、有耐性和持之以恒、百折不挠的精神。千万不能今天十二分努力，而明天便一式也不练，一曝十寒，三天打鱼、两天晒网，这是永远学不好的。

（2）不松懈：不管严寒酷暑都不能间断，甚至在紧张而繁忙的学习或工作时间，也必须抽出时间来练一练，经常不断地练才能从太极拳中获益。

（3）要专心：学拳的人都有一个通病，便是贪多。要知道各种拳理本来相通，一通就百通。否则一样不精,就是学了一百套也是没有用的,反之精通了一套也就等于精通了百套。

（4）不急于求成：练功,宁可渐进,不可过急,欲速则不达。拳术的功夫是快不来的,练一天是一天的工夫,学一天有一天的成绩。急于求成是不可能的。万丈高楼要从平地起,不是一朝一夕所能筑成。

除此之外,还应请有经验的老师做正确的指导,"先入为主",如果在初学时即走了弯路,那么想拐回来再走正路往往要费很大的工夫,需改正错误动作技术再学习新的。在练拳或学拳时,如无人指导又想要知道所做的姿势是否正确,下列简单方法可以自行检查和纠正：在动作时,如感觉上体、胸、背部、上肢等部位都很舒适并呼吸自然,而下肢腿(尤其大腿)特别吃力负重,表明姿势是正确的；反之如感觉上肢僵硬有力,胸、背部又有截气和瘀闷不舒的现象,下肢腿部不觉吃力,并且有浮而飘、不稳定等状态发生,这就是姿势不够正确的表现。这是简单可行的自我衡量太极拳动作姿势是否正确的尺度,也是练好太极拳的自我保障。

三、简化太极拳动作路线图

如图 6-1 所示为简化太极拳动作路线图。

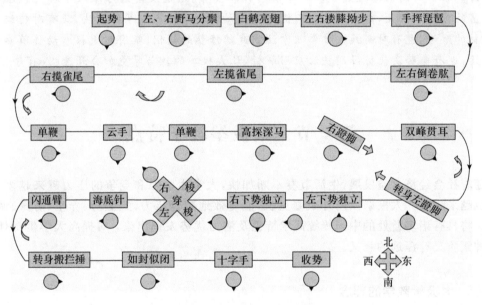

图 6-1　简化太极拳动作路线图

第七章　太极拳的教学特点与学练方法

> 太极拳作为我国武术传统项目中的宝贵文化遗产之一,形式柔和缓慢,动作圆活连绵不断,动静相济,柔中寓刚,既可以强身健体,又可以在必要时防身自卫,还适合于体弱多病者作为医疗保健和康复练习的手段,也是普及、推广全民健身运动的项目之一。由于太极拳的特点是以内引外、顺势自如、虚实分明、连绵不断,相对于其他的体育运动项目,有其特定的教学难度,而且传统教学方式教学往往周期较长,不适于课时较短的大学本科教学。本书在太极教学内容方面进行了补充,突出了太极基本功和内功的修炼内容,以便使初学者能在短时间内掌握太极拳的基本动作和要领,通过反复练习深入了解太极理论及其丰富的内涵。因此,本章内容专门探讨太极拳的教学特点与学练方法,既有对传统太极拳教材的改进,也有对新式太极拳教学注重武德修养的提倡;既有对太极拳动作节奏的规律揭示,也有拳势变化练习的技法应用解析,让太极拳的教与学更加公开透明、有序合理。

第一节　太极拳教学特点

随着社会经济日益发展,生活节奏不断加快,大学生学习和竞争的压力越来越多,心理负担也越来越重。太极拳以内外兼修见长,能有效地减轻压力,集健身、养生、防身、调心为一体。将具有诸多益处的中国传统武术特色及潜力优势发掘出来,对提高大学生身体素质和精神素质具有深远的意义。

一、太极拳教学的理念

本书提倡的太极拳教学理念,是"整体育人"思想。其核心教学目标是变"演武"为"研武",变"练拳"为"练全"。不仅使学生在课上得到锻炼,而且通过教学,使学生领悟武术运动及太极拳的基本理论知识,帮助学生掌握正确的运动技能和科学锻炼身体的方法,培养其坚持锻炼的习惯和热情,逐渐养成健康积极的生活方式,使学生终身受益。

高校太极拳教学,应致力于从根本上提高学生的学习质量和生活质量,特别注重武德教育和大学生的身心全面发展,帮助学生尽快了解武术传统文化,最终形成独具特色的个人武术健身与修身风格,符合当代素质教育的基本要求。

二、太极拳教学的特点

太极拳教学与常规体育教学相比,其民族传统特色尤显突出,体现在现代与传统、体育与文化的交融,既强调健体养生,又注重心理承受能力及应变能力等综合素质的有效提高。

太极拳教学,有着不同于其他体育项目的特点。除了外部的技巧训练,特别强调武术文化的传承、内部修为的技法、养生之道等方面。"练拳必须明理",尤其是现代大学生习武,除了练习拳脚功夫,更重要的是自我意识的发展。本书的教学内容侧重弘扬民族武术文化精髓,培育学生的民族意识和民族气质,培养他们的组织性、纪律性、勇敢坚毅的品格和集体主义精神,引导学生追求生活的真谛:积极人生、健康人生,使学生从理论到实践对中国武术文化形成一个系统的认识。

太极拳教学应从传统武术入手,通过教学,使学生在课上得到锻炼,从而使他们领悟武术运动的基本理论知识,掌握正确的武术技能和实战防身方法。把习练太极拳过程中悟到的生命精髓付诸生活实践中,重新认识自我,缓解生活压力,超越自我,增强自信,充分发挥每个人的潜能,特别强调武术文化的传承和内在修为,重视身心和谐发展,实现"整体育人"。强调对现代社会中自救防身意识和方法的指导,可有效地提高学生应对突发事件的能力。

太极拳是我国宝贵的民族传统体育项目,太极拳课程也是高校体育课教学的重要内容之一。本书的教学目标为弘扬民族武术文化精髓,并与中国武术段位制接轨,对上课礼仪也有特定的要求。教学内容亦包括传统中国太极功夫特有的教学训练手段以及太极文化和哲理的交互融入等。

三、太极拳教学应注重武德修养

武德修养,就是按照武德原则、规范进行一系列自我反省、自我认识、自我批评、自我改造的过程,以及经过长期努力所形成的高尚的情操和道德境界。我们现在讲的武德修养,主要是指习武者在政治、道德及技艺等方面所进行的勤奋学习和锻炼的功夫,以及经过长期努力达到的一种思想品质和能力。

道德修养是中华民族的优良传统,而武德修养作为一种重要的道德修养,主张用"养气""内求"的修养方法培养所谓的"至大至刚"和立于天地之间的"浩然正气"。在今天,更应该重视继承中华民族的修养传统,强调武德修养对人们道德品质的重要意义,使人们意识到,经过刻苦修养和锻炼,都可以达到较高的道德境界,进而提高自己各方面的素质。

武德修养包含以下十个方面的基本内容。

(1) 武德高——爱国爱民,品德高尚。

为武之道,以德为本。习武者首先要重视武德的学习,要有好的思想品质,这是提高武技的前提。

(2) 武旨正——强身健体,卫国防身。

学习武术的宗旨要正确,练武是为了强健身体,掌握武技为人民服务、保卫国家和人民安全,绝非恃艺为非作歹,损害群众利益。

(3) 武纪严——不斗凶狠,遵规守纪。

有了一定的武术技能,不能逞凶斗狠,无事生非,应该遵守各项法规制度,做遵纪守法的模范,并能够主动同坏人做斗争。

(4) 武风良——尊师爱生,互研拳学。

在武林同人中,要形成一种老师爱护学生,学生尊敬老师,互相尊重,共同研习武术的良好风气,为武术的发展贡献出一分力量。

(5) 武礼谦——抱拳行礼,谦和礼貌。

无论习武者之间,还是与其他人之间,都应该以礼相待、有礼有节、平易近人、谦虚诚恳,不能出口不逊、得意忘形、败坏武德。

(6) 武志坚——意志坚强,百折不挠。

武术,是一项内容繁多、技术较高的运动项目,学习起来有一定难度,这就要求习武者要坚强有意志,不怕困难,立志为武术事业献身。

(7) 武学勤——拳不离手,勤学苦练。

要学习好武术,就应该拳不离手,坚持不懈地朝演夕练、勤学苦练。历史上武术有所成就的人,都是勤学的结果,只有这样才能学习好武术。

(8) 武技精——钻研武技,精益求精。

艺无止境,武术博大精深、内涵丰富,非一朝一夕所能穷尽,必须刻苦钻研、不断进取、精益求精,才能武艺精湛。

(9) 武仪端——举止庄重,容端体正。

习武者应该仪表端正、举止文雅,表现出气宇轩昂的精神风貌,不能衣装不整、体态不端。

(10) 武境美——环境优美,井然有序。

练习武术,要主动保持练习场地、生活环境的卫生,特别是训练场地、衣物、器件等要摆放整齐,爱护公物,让习武环境、生活环境优美整洁。

此外,武德修养还体现在重视和遵循武礼规范上,武术行礼规范的基本方式包括以下几种。

(1) 抱拳礼。

图 7-1

太极拳中的礼法很多,"抱拳礼"是现今武术的规定,是国内外一致被采用的具有代表性的礼法。此礼法是由中国传统"作揖礼"和少林拳的抱拳礼(四指礼),加以提炼、规范、统一得来的,并赋予了新的含义。行礼的方法是:并步站立,左手四指并拢伸直成掌,拇指屈拢,右手成拳,左掌心掩贴右掌面(左指根线与右拳棱相齐),左指尖与下颏平齐,右掌眼(虎口)斜对胸窝,置于胸前屈臂成圆,肘尖略下垂,拳掌与胸相距20~30厘米,头正,身直,目视受礼者,面容举止自然大方,如图7-1所示。晚辈(或学生)施"抱拳礼"可同时问"您好"或"老师好"。

(2) 点首礼。

受礼者并步直立,目视施礼者微微点头示意,勿低头弯腰。此系受礼者表示对施礼者答诺的一种礼仪。一般长辈(师长)对晚辈(生徒)施此礼节。同学、平辈间也可采用。平时见面礼,不分辈分也可用此礼。

(3) 注目礼。

施礼者并步站立,目视受礼者或向前平视。勿点头弯腰。这是表示对受礼者的恭敬、尊重的礼仪。

崇德尚武,发扬民族精神,是今天我们所提倡武德的基本原则。武德在发展过程中,从最初维护民族利益的道德观,到现在把国家、民族的利益放在首位,冲破单一、狭隘的道德意识,终于使尚武与道德紧密结合,构成了中国民族精神的主体。崇德是尚武的前提,尚武是崇德的反映,通过崇德尚武,最终要发扬"自强不息""厚德载物"的民族精神,为社会做出贡献。

第二节　太极拳学练方法

一、太极拳教学的基本步骤

由于太极拳的动作名称较多,为了方便记忆,本书仅以简化二十四式太极拳为例,将部分动作、名称进行压缩,如:分鬃及亮翅,即左、右野马分鬃及白鹤亮翅动作;雀尾单鞭及云手,即是左、右揽雀尾单鞭及云手的运作等。

1. 正确理解动作要领

太极拳的整套基本动作是以头颈正直,下颏微向后收,动作连绵不断,动静分明,不忽高忽低(左、右下势独立动作除外),不要故意挺胸或收腹,两肩下沉,两肘松垂,手指自然微屈,精神要集中。

2. 熟记歌诀和动作顺序

起势分鬃及亮翅,拗步琵琶倒卷肱。
雀尾单鞭加云手,探马蹬腿贯耳捶。
下势穿梭捞海底,闪通转身搬拦捶。
如封似闭十字手,收势方向要记清。

3. 重复动作练习,掌握变化规律,提高学习兴趣

如在第一组动作中的左、右野马分鬃,可把它简化成为一个左野马分鬃来进行练习,而右野马分鬃只是方向不同而已;在第二组左、右搂膝拗步推掌中,当掌握了左搂膝拗步推掌的动作后,右搂膝拗步推掌的动作也就学会了,因为它的动作也和上面例子一样,只不过是左或右方向不同罢了。

再就是段落分部合并:如第一组中的左、右野马分鬃到白鹤亮翅,至第二组中的左、右搂膝拗步推掌到手挥琵琶动作的步法完全一样,它们只是上肢动作不同,腿部动作完全一样,所以,步法可合并,只要练习上肢动作就行。又如,左、右倒卷肱动作,它只有一个动作,但重复做四次而已,不同之处只是左右交替、手脚调换罢了,所以学会一个倒卷肱动作就能领会其他倒卷肱动作。其他类似重复动作同样可按照以上方法进行合并。

4. 变换动作节奏和顺序,提高熟练程度

对初学者来说,往往由于太极拳的动作缓慢而失去学习的兴趣,鉴于年轻人好胜心强的心理特点,为了让初学者能对太极拳产生兴趣,在对动作还不熟练的时候,本书提倡可以适当提高原来动作的频率和速度,这样既可以在很大程度上解决动作概念模糊的问题,又可以

排除厌倦和烦躁的心理。在课堂上实行这种方法,深受大学生欢迎,教学效果非常好。

5. 进行太极拳拳势变化练习,掌握太极拳的基本技法应用

初学者按太极拳的动作、技术要求进行练习,特别强调在演练时做到心静用意、意动形随、柔刚相济、内外合一,亦即意识、动作、呼吸三者同时协调地运动,用其以静御动、虽动犹静、气宜鼓荡的精髓来调理身体。转动时要以腰脊为轴,松腰、松胯;两臂随腰运转,自然、圆活速度缓慢均匀、下肢移动时,重心要稳定,眼的视线随左右手而移动;呼吸自然等。

二、学会看技术图解——"武术技术图解的方法及其应用"

太极拳图解是记载太极拳动作和套路的重要方式,它由文字说明和插图两部分组成。文字说明讲解动作的详细过程、方法和要领。插图描绘动作姿势和身体各部位(包括器械)的运动路线和方向。

正确掌握太极拳图解知识,便于自学,对自修能力的培养和较好地理解技术动作,提高技术水平有着重要意义。同时,运用图解知识来记载太极拳动作和套路,有利于交流、推广、继承和发展,对促进中华太极拳的发扬光大起着积极的作用。太极拳图解包括运动方向、运动路线、往返路线、叙述顺序、动作名称和要领说明等方面。

1. 运动方向

图解中的运动方向,是以图中人的躯干姿势为准,并随着躯干姿势所处的位置变化而变化。图中人的身前为前、身后为后、左侧为左、右侧为右,向地心为下,离地心为上;此外,还有左前、左后、右前、右后、左上、左下、右上、右下之分。转体时,则以转后的身前为前,身后为后,以此类推。如各种套路开始的预备势,前后左右的方向是以图中人体躯干姿势为准。

如图 7-2 所示,身前为前、背后为后、左侧为左、右侧为右;如图 7-3 所示,九式太极操作中的左螺旋缠绕式是以身体左转后的前方为前、背后为后。

图 7-2

图 7-3

有时也有用东、南、西、北的写法表示方向,这和看地图的方向是一致的。太极拳的动作多而复杂,身体变化较大,但始终以躯干姿势来确定方向,不受头部和视线的影响。

2. 运动路线

太极拳图中一般用虚线(┄┄▸)和实线(──▸)表示该部位下一个动作将要进行的路线。箭头为止点,箭尾为起点。实线与虚线,分别表示左右边,一般左虚右实,如九式太极操的"把球开合式"(如图7-4所示),其运动路线就是遵循"左虚右实"的原则。

但有的插图右上肢和左下肢用实线表示,左上肢和右下肢用虚线表示;有的上、下肢分别用虚线和实线来表示(如图7-5所示)。

图 7-4

图 7-5

此外,有的图中还标出了足迹图,用来表示脚在运动中的路线变化。虽然用法不一,但作用都是相同的,都是表明下一运动将进行的路线。

3. 往返路线

太极拳套路是由若干段(趟)构成,各段的往返路线,一般是单数段向左,双数段则转向原来的右侧方向。弄清每段的前进方向之后,即使在前进中有转身的动作变化,转身后仍朝着原来的方向前进。这样每段的方向就不容易搞错。在学习比较复杂的套路时,每段的前进方向经常变化,这时可采用化整为零的方法,将一段分成若干小节来学习。套路的起势和收势应在同一方向,并且位置接近,如果练习中出现方向相反或不能基本还原,说明练习中运动方向出现了错误,则应对照图解,逐一检查和纠正。

4. 叙述顺序

文字叙述过程中,一般先写下肢(步型、步法、腿法等),继之写明运动方向(向前、向后、向左、向右等),再写上肢动作(手型、手法、肘法、持器械方法及运动方法),最后注明目视方向。个别情况下,也有以身体各部位运动的先后顺序来写。另外,文字说明中有"左(右)"或"右(左)"的写法,表示左右均可或左右互换的意思;有"同时"的写法,则表示无论先写或后写的身体各部位都应一齐运动,如上、下肢同时运动,先写下肢后写上肢。

5. 动作名称

为简化文字说明,方便记忆与交流,太极拳图解常使用动作名称。动作名称多以下肢的主要动作结合上肢的主要动作来命名,例如,马步顶肘、弓步冲拳、提膝刺剑、歇步劈刀等。有的根据动作形象命名,例如白鹤亮翅、手挥琵琶、乌龙盘打、金鸡独立等。掌握动作名称的含义,有利于帮助我们阅读图解和理解动作。

6. 要领说明

有些太极拳图解中,在动作的后面附有"要领"或"要点"之类的文字说明,提示该动作的技术要领,或者说明应注意之处。例如,"冲拳"的要领是拧腰、顺肩、急旋臂;弓步的要领是前弓、后蹬、挺胸、立腰等。阅读时须认真领会,只有掌握了要领,并反复练习才能正确地完成该动作。

三、练习太极拳套路的三个阶段

步法和单个动作的练习是练好太极拳的基础。有武谚曰:未习拳先习步,未练武先练桩。可见步型、步法的重要。步型、步法的学习看似简单,所以易被初学者忽视。步型、步法是稳定中心的关键,步型不正确、步法不得当都会造成重心不稳。如迈步过小、过窄,出脚的位置、方向、角度不对,都会形成上身不正、重心不稳等现象。所以,步型要准确,出步要适度,前进、后退、左顾、右盼、中定,始终保持百会穴与会阴穴在一条垂直线上。正如太极拳理论所讲:"无过不及,随屈就伸,立如标杆,活似车轮。"因此步型、步法的练习有利于下盘动作的稳定性及培养身型、步法的协调性,可为进一步学习太极拳打下基础。

初学太极拳时不要贪多求快,潦草从事,如果贪多求快造成错误的定型,再进行纠正就困难了。错误的姿势如臀部外凸,就会牵连出现腰和胸的前挺、腹肌紧张等问题,不但对身体无益,对将来提高拳艺也是大敌。因此,初学者应该从基础学起,从单个动作一招一式地认真学起。以二十四式简化太极拳为例,如左、右野马分鬃,左、右搂膝拗步,左、右倒卷肱,左、右揽雀尾,左、右云手,左、右下式独立,左、右穿梭,均可提取出来单独练习。逐一练习这些单势,不但便于"动作定型",而且有助于专心体会动作细节。这些单势动作是套路的核心、骨架,练好了就等于构筑好了套路立架。从健身效果看,单式重复亦能达到预期效果,单式动作同样涵盖了完整套路的要领和作用。因此,初学者不要贪多求快,要耐心体会每一单式的要领和感受,做到学会一式、掌握一式,并能够运用这一式进行健身锻炼。单式练习还有一个便利因素,即不受时间、场地的约束,无论室内、室外、时间长短,少则左右重复三五遍,多则数十遍,总能随心所欲,真所谓"拳打立脚之地"。把这些单个动作练纯熟以后,就可以学习完整的套路了。

在掌握了步法与单个动作后,就可以结合一些过渡动作学习简化太极拳的套路了。在练习套路时,可分成三个阶段来练习。

1. 塑形

在塑形阶段首先要讲究立身端正,心静体松。所谓"端正",就是体要正直、中正,不可前俯后仰、左右歪斜,要保持尾闾和脊椎呈一直线,始终处于端正状态。在练习太极拳时要抓住姿势"端正"这一重要环节,立身端正才能稳住下盘重心。初学时可能会出现动作死板与不够灵活的现象，但是只要勤学苦练，就能由拙变巧，在中正的基础上求圆匀。所谓"心静"，就是心平气静；"体松"就是身体舒展。在练习过程中，思想上要尽量排除一切杂念，心理上始终保持安静状态，把精神贯注到每个细小的动作上去，做到专心练拳，肌肉、关节、韧带都尽量处于自然舒展的状态，使其不受任何拘束或压迫。

2. 匀劲

当大脑逐步建立了完整正确的技术动作概念，形体外表符合太极拳的技术要求，即动作规范、立身端正、心静、体松、套路熟练、达到自如的程度时，就应当注意动作的匀劲。要使动作表现出匀劲，必须注意"连贯圆活""上下相随"两个方面的练习。"圆活"就是动作不能直来直去，练习时动作要做得灵活自然、衔接活顺，动作路线能按不同的弧线反复交换。在动作要领上要特别注意由腰背带动四肢进行活动，体会转腰、旋臂、松肩、垂肘、屈膝、松胯。"连贯"是指各动作之间都前后衔接，不可出现停顿、突变和断续的痕迹。全套动作要势势相连、运转不停，犹如春蚕吐丝、绵绵不断，像行云流水相连无间，节节贯穿，一气呵成。"上下相随"指的是上肢、下肢和躯干等各部的配合要协调一致，上下连贯，手腕相随，周身协调、完整；运动时，必须根于脚，发于腿，主宰于腰而行于手指，由脚而腿而腰须完整一气，腰背领动，手脚随动，眼神随之，浑然一体。针对这段练习首先应该先从理论入手，阅读有关太极拳理论方面的书刊，再观看一些名人的太极拳录像带，尽量多了解太极拳术的特点、方法以及练习要领。其次，反复练习套路，由感性练习上升到理性练习，逐步使动作走出匀劲。

3. 求意

求意阶段是练好简化太极拳的最高阶段。在本阶段的练习中，主要强调意识与呼吸、动作的协调一致，故有"意、气、神合一"之说。而呼吸自然、虚实分明是求意过程中不可缺少的两大要领。因为"柔、匀、细、长"的腹式呼吸符合太极拳动作要求。在太极拳运动中有一个根本原则就是"顺应自然，吸满当呼，呼尽当吸，呼吸均匀"。根据太极拳运动的特点，大体上是"起吸落呼，开吸合呼"，通常在完成两臂上伸外展、扩胸、提肩、展体时吸气，完成与上述动作相反时呼气。太极拳里所说的"虚"就是灵活松软的意思，"实"就是紧张、坚实的意思。虚是松、实是紧，虚实在太极拳动作中是相辅相成、相互制约的，是矛盾的对立统一。从动作上来讲，一般上动作结束的定势为"实"，动作变换过程为"虚"；发劲为"实"，蓄劲为"虚"；支撑体重腿为"实"，移动换劲腿为"虚"；体现动作内容的手臂为"实"，辅助动作配合的手臂为"虚"。分清了动作的虚实，在练习中就能有张有弛，区别对待。当然，这个规定不是在任何情况下都适用的，因为太极拳的走劲形式变化多端。有时出手蓄劲，收手发劲；有时沉降落劲，提升发劲；有时连续发劲或连续蓄劲，即连续数次走化敌意、借以争势、伺机而发等。那么，什么时候当"实"，什么时候当"虚"，应以行为中的真意为准，方能完成好动作，使意识、呼吸与动作能巧妙自然相合，做到虚中有实、实中有虚、刚柔相济、轻灵沉稳、势换劲连、劲换意连。

四、练习太极拳的关键

1. 心静体松

所谓"心静"，就是在练习太极拳时，思想上应排除一切杂念，不受外界干扰；所谓"体松"，可不是全身松懈疲沓，而是指在练拳时保持身体姿势正确的基础上，有意识地让全身关节、肌肉以及内脏等达到最大限度的放松状态。

2. 圆活连贯

"心静体松"是对太极拳练习的基本要求。而是否做到"圆活连贯"才是衡量一个人功夫深浅的主要依据。太极拳练习所要求的"连贯"是指多方面的。其一是指肢体的连贯，即所谓的"节节贯穿"。肢体的连贯是以腰为枢纽的。在动作转换过程中，则要求：对下肢，是以腰带胯，以胯带膝，以膝带足；对上肢，是以腰带背，以背带肩，以肩带肘，再以肘带手。其二是动作与动作之间的衔接，即"势势相连"——前一动作的结束就是下一个动作的开始，势势之间没有间断和停顿。而"圆活"是在连贯基础上的进一步要求，意指活顺、自然。

3. 虚实分明

要做到"运动如抽丝，迈步似猫行"，首先要注意虚实变换要适当，是肢体各部在运动中没有丝毫不稳定的现象。若不能维持平衡稳定，就根本谈不上什么"迈步如猫行"了。一般来说，下肢以主要支撑体重的腿为实，辅助支撑或移动换步的腿为虚；上肢以体现动作主要内容的手臂为实，辅助配合的手臂为虚。总之，虚实不但要互相渗透，还需在意识指导下变化灵活。

4. 呼吸自然

太极拳联系的呼吸方法有自然呼吸、腹式顺呼吸、腹式逆呼吸和拳式呼吸。以上几种呼吸方法，不论采用哪一种，都应自然、匀细，徐徐吞吐，要与动作自然配合。初学者采用自然呼吸。

附录一　古传《太极拳论》及经典歌诀

一、王宗岳《太极拳论》

太极拳论

王宗岳

太极者，无极而生，动静之机，阴阳之母也。动之则分，静之则合。无过不及，随屈就伸。人刚我柔谓之走，我顺人背谓之粘。动急则急应，动缓则缓随。虽变化万端，而理唯一贯。由着熟而渐悟懂劲，由懂劲而阶及神明。然非用力之久，不能豁然贯通焉。

虚灵顶劲，气沉丹田。不偏不倚，忽隐忽现。左重则左虚，右重则右杳。仰之则弥高，俯之则弥深，进之则愈长，退之则愈促，一羽不能加，蝇虫不能落，人不知我，我独知人。英雄所向无敌，盖皆由此而及也。

斯技旁门甚多，虽势有区别，概不外壮欺弱慢让快耳。"有力打无力，手慢让手快"，是皆先天自然之能，非关学力而后有也。察"四两拨千斤"之句，显非力胜！观耄耋御众之形，快何能为！

立如平准，活似车轮，偏沉则随，双重则滞。每见数年纯功不能运化者，率皆自为人制；双重之病未悟耳。

欲避此病，须知阴阳；粘即是走，走即是粘。阴不离阳，阳不离阴；阴阳相济，方为懂劲。懂劲而后，愈练愈精，默识揣摩，渐至从心所欲。本是舍己从人，多误舍近求远；所谓"差之毫厘，谬以千里"。学者不可不详辨焉，是为论。

（引自《太极拳涵化文集》，王子和辑录。）

二、杨澄甫《太极拳说十要》

太极拳说十要

杨澄甫口述　陈微明录

（1）虚灵顶劲

顶劲者，头容正直，神贯于顶也。不可用力，用力则项强，气血不能流通。须有虚灵自然之意。非有虚灵顶劲，则精神不能提起也。

（2）含胸拔背

含胸者，胸略内涵，使气沉于丹田也。胸忌挺出，挺出则气涌胸际，上重下轻，脚跟易于浮起。拔背者，气贴于背也。能含胸，则自能拔背；能拔背，则能力由脊发，所向无敌也。

（3）松腰

腰为一身之主宰，能松腰然后两足有力，下盘稳固。虚实变化，皆由腰转动，故曰："命意源头在腰隙""有不得力,必于腰腿求之"也。

（4）分虚实

太极拳术以分虚实为第一义。如全身皆坐在右腿,则右腿为实,左腿为虚;全身坐在左腿,则左腿为实,右腿为虚。虚实能分,而后转动轻灵,毫不费力。如不能分,则迈步重滞,自立不稳,而易为人所牵动。

（5）沉肩坠肘

沉肩者,肩松开下垂也。若不能松垂,两肩端起,则气亦随之而上,全身皆不得力矣。坠肘者,肘往下松坠之意。肘若悬起,则肩不能沉,放人不远,近于外家之断劲矣。

（6）用意不用力

太极拳论云:"此全是用意不用力。"练太极拳,全身松开,不使有分毫之拙劲,以留滞于筋骨血脉之间,以自缚束。然后能轻灵变化,圆转自如。

或疑不用力何以能长力?盖人身之有经络,如地之有沟壑。沟壑不塞而水行,经络不闭而气通。如浑身僵劲充满经络,气血停滞,转动不灵,牵一发而全身动矣。若不用力而用意,意之所至,气即至焉。如是气血流注,日日贯输,周流全身,无时停滞。久久练习,则得真正内劲。即太极拳论所云:"极柔软,然后极坚刚"也。

太极拳功夫纯熟之人,臂膊如绵裹铁,分量极沉。练外家拳者,用力则显有力,不用力时,则甚轻浮。可见其力,乃外劲浮面之劲也。不用意而用力,最易引动,不足尚也。

（7）上下相随

上下相随者,即太极拳论所云:"其根在脚,发于腿,主宰于腰,形于手指,由脚而腿而腰,总须完整一气"也。手动,腰动,足动,眼神亦随之动。如是方可谓之"上下相随"。有一不动,即散乱也。

（8）内外相合

太极拳所练在神。故云:"神为主帅,身为驱使。"精神能提得起,自然举动轻灵。架子不外虚实开合。所谓开者,不但手足开,心意与之俱开;所谓合者,不但手足合,心意亦与之俱合。能内外合为一气,则浑然无间矣。

（9）相连不断

外家拳术,其劲乃后天之拙劲。故有起有止,有续有断。旧力已尽,新力未生,此时最易为人所乘。太极拳用意不用力,自始至终,绵绵不断,周而复始,循环无穷。原论所谓"如长江大海,滔滔不绝",又曰:"运劲如抽丝",皆言其贯串一气也。

（10）动中求静

外家拳术,以跳掷为能,用尽气力,故练习之后,无不喘气者。太极拳以静御动,虽动犹静,故练架子愈慢愈好。慢则呼吸深长,气沉丹田,自无血脉贲张之弊。学者细心体会,庶可得其意焉。

三、《十三势歌》

十三势歌

十三总势莫轻视,命意源头在腰隙。
变换虚实需留意,气遍身躯不稍滞。
静中触动动尤静,因敌变化示神奇。

势势存心揆用意,得来不觉费功夫。
刻刻留心在腰间,腹内松净气腾然。
尾闾中正神贯顶,满身轻利顶头悬。
仔细留心向推求,屈伸开合听自由。
入门引路需口授,功用无息法自修。
若言体用何为准,意气君来骨肉臣。
想推用意终何在,益寿延年不老春。
歌兮歌兮百四十,字字真切义无遗。
若不向此推求去,枉费功夫贻叹息。

四、《十三势行功心解》

十三势行功心解

王宗岳

　　以心行气,务令沉着,乃能收敛入骨。以气运身,务令顺遂,乃能便利从心。精神能提得起,则无迟重之虞,所谓顶头悬也。意气须换得灵,乃有圆活之趣,所谓变动虚实也。发劲须沉着松静,专注一方。立身须中正安舒,支撑八面。

　　行气如九曲珠,无微不到。运劲如百炼钢,无坚不摧。形如搏兔之鹘,神如捕鼠之猫。静如山岳,动若江河。蓄劲如张弓,发劲如放箭。曲中求直,蓄而后发。力由脊发,步随身换。收即是放,断而复连。往复须有折叠,进退须有转换。极柔软,然后极坚刚。能呼吸,然后能灵活。气以直养而无害,劲以曲蓄而有余。心为令,气为旗,腰为纛。先求开展,后求紧凑。乃可臻于缜密矣!

　　又曰:先在心,后在身。腰松净气敛入骨,神舒体静。刻刻在心。切记"一动无有不动,一静无有不静。"牵动往来气贴背,敛入脊骨。内固精神,外示安逸。迈步如猫行,运劲如抽丝。全身意在精神,不在气。在气则滞。有气者无力,无气者纯刚。气若车轮,腰如车轴。

五、《打手歌》

打手歌

王宗岳修订

掤捋挤按须认真,上下相随人难进。
任他巨力来打我,牵动四两拨千斤。
引进落空合即出,粘黏连随不丢顶。

六、《八字歌》

八字歌

(相传为唐许宣平所传太极功之要诀)
掤捋挤按世间稀,十个艺人十不知。
若能轻灵并坚硬,粘黏连随俱无疑。
采挒肘靠更出奇,行之不用费心思。
果得粘黏连随字,得其环中不支离。

七、《周身大用歌》

周身大用歌

（相传为唐许宣平所传太极功之要诀）

一要心灵与意静，自然无处不轻灵。

二要遍体气流行，一定继续不能停。

三要喉头永不抛，问尽天下众英豪。

如询大用缘何得，表里精粗无不到。

八、《十六关要诀》

十六关要诀

（相传为唐许宣平所传太极功之要诀）

活泼于腰，灵机于顶，神通于背，流行于气。

行之于腿，蹬之于足，运之于掌，通之于指。

敛之于髓，达之于神，凝之于耳，息之于鼻。

呼吸往来于口，纵之于膝，浑噩于身，全身发之于毛。

（引自赵斌、赵又斌、路迪民著．杨代太极拳真传[M]．北京：北京体育大学出版社，2011年8月1日第2版．）

附录二　武术（太极拳）段位入段指南

第一条　目的

为增强人民体质,推动武术运动的发展,提高武术技术和理论水平,建立规范的全民武术体系,特制定本段位制。

第二条　段位名称

根据个人从事武术锻炼和武术活动的年限,掌握武术技术和理论的水平、研究成果、武德修养,以及对武术发展所做出的贡献,将武术段位定为九段。设:

初段位:一段、二段、三段

中段位:四段、五段、六段

高段位:七段、八段、九段

第三条　晋段标准

(一)初段位的晋升

1. 凡参加武术套路基础锻炼年满8岁或参加武术散手基础训练年满13周岁(仅限男子),入段资格技术考评成绩达7分以上,并接受武德教育者,可取得入段资格。

2. 凡取得入段资格达1年以上,在规定的考评中,演练一段的一套拳术或散手基础技术,成绩达7.5分以上,遵守武德者,可申请晋升一段。

3. 凡获得一段达1年以上,在规定的考评中,演练二段的一套拳术,成绩达8分以上,或在散手攻防组合技术考评中,成绩达8分以上,遵守武德者,可申请晋升二段。

4. 凡获得二段达1年以上,在规定的考评中,演练三段的一套拳术、一套器械(长短任选),每项成绩达8.5分以上,或在散手实战技术考评中,成绩达8.5分以上,遵守武德者,可申请晋升三段。

(二)中段位的晋升

1. 凡获得三段达2年以上,符合下列条件之一者,可晋升四段:

(1) 在规定的考评中,演练四段的一套拳术、一套短器械、一套长器械,总成绩达25.8分以上,并在该段的武术理论考试中,成绩达到75分以上,重视武德修养者;

(2) 在规定的散手四段晋段比赛考评中,成绩达到规定录取名次,并在该段的武术理论考试中,成绩达到75分以上,重视武德修养者。

2. 凡获得四段达2年以上,符合下列条件之一者,可申报晋升五段:

(1) 在规定的套路晋级比赛考评中,演练一套拳术、一套短器械、一套长器械或二套拳术、一套器械(仅限于太极拳系列),其中一项达到规定录取名次,成绩达到26.25分以上,并在该段位的武术理论考试中,成绩达到80分以上,重视武德修养者;

(2) 在规定的散手五段晋级比赛考评中,成绩达到规定录取名次,并在该段的武术理论考评中,成绩达到80分以上,重视武德修养者。

3. 凡获得五段达 2 年以上,符合下列条件之一者,可申报晋升六段:

(1) 在规定的套路晋级比赛考评中,演练六段的一套拳术、一套短器械、一套长器械或二套拳术、一套对练(仅限于太极拳系列),其中一项达到规定录取名次,成绩达到 27 分以上,并在该段位的武术理论考试中,成绩达到 85 分以上,重视武德修养者;

(2) 在规定的散手六段晋级比赛考评中,成绩达到规定录取名次,并在该段的武术理论考评中,成绩达到 85 分以上,重视武德修养者。

(三) 高段位的晋升

1. 凡获得六段达 6 年以上,在工作业绩、武术理论研究、科研论著中取得一定成绩,武德高尚者,可申请晋升七段。

2. 凡获得七段达 5 年以上,在工作业绩、武术理论研究、科研论著中取得一定成绩,并对武术运动的发展做出较大贡献,武德高尚者,可申请晋升八段。

3. 凡获得八段以后,在工作业绩、武术科研论著、理论研究方面取得重大成就,并对武术运动的发展做出卓越贡献,影响极大,武德高尚者,可申请晋升九段。

4. 对武术事业的发展做出卓越贡献的知名人士,经国家体委武术运动管理中心审核后,可授予荣誉高段位。

第四条 申报、考评与审批办法

(一) 凡遵守武德,热爱武术,具有相应的武术技术和理论水平,均可申报武术段位。只有国家体委武术运动管理中心授权的各级考评委员会,才有权组织考评。

(二) 各区、县武术考评委员会,每年对基层武术组织的学员进行套路或散手入段资格技术和一段的考评,并将考评合格者的申报材料上报所在区、县体委主管部门(或武术协会)审批,授予入段资格证明或相应的段位。

(三) 地、市体委段位考评委员会,每年可举行二段和三段的考评,并将考评合格者的申报材料上报所在地、市体委武术主管部门(或武术协会)审批,授予相应的段位。

(四) 省、自治区、直辖市体委及行业体协武术段位考评委员会,每年举行四段、五段和六段的考评,并将考评合格者的申报材料上报所在省、自治区、直辖市体委,及行业体协武术主管部门(或武术协会)审批,授予相应的段位。

(五) 全国武术段位考评委员会将适时组织七段、八段和九段的评审,并将评审合格者的申报材料,上报国家体委武术运动管理中心审批,授予相应的段位。

(六) 各段位的考评形式包括:1. 省级和全国性的各类武术比赛;2. 规定的段位晋升考评。

第五条 证书、服装与徽饰

(一) 证书

由国家体委武术运动管理中心统一设计、制作。

(二) 服装

由国家体委武术运动管理中心统一设计,指定专门厂家制作。

(三) 徽饰

由国家体委武术运动管理中心统一设计,指定专门厂家制作。

1. 初段位:一段(青鹰);二段(银鹰);三段(金鹰)

2. 中段位:四段(青虎);五段(银虎);六段(金虎)

3. 高段位:七段(青龙);八段(银龙);九段(金龙)

附录三　太极拳竞赛规则

场地与装备

第一部分　场地①

《全国武术套路竞赛规则》对太极拳套路比赛的场地做出了具体规定：

——个人项目的场地为长 14 米、宽 8 米，其周围至少有 2 米宽的安全区。
——集体项目的场地为长 16 米、宽 14 米，其周围至少有 1 米宽的安全区。
——场地四周内沿，应标明 5 厘米宽的白色边线。
——场地的地面空间高度不低于 8 米。
——两个比赛场地之间的距离 6 米以上。
——根据实际情况比赛场地应高出地面 50～60 厘米。
——场地灯光垂直照度和水平照度在规定范围之内。

场地示意图（如图 1、图 2 所示）②：

全场比赛裁判席位图

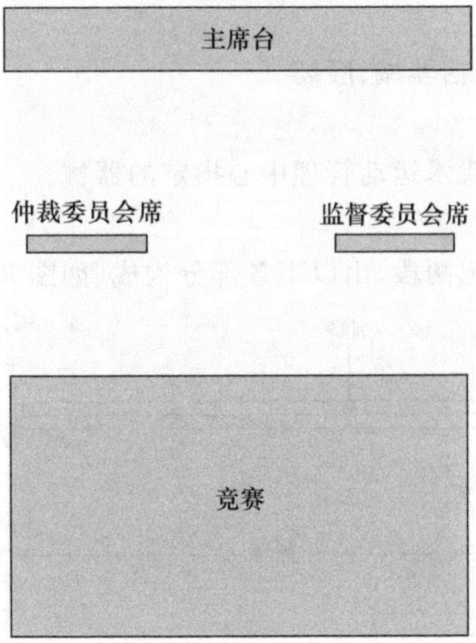

主席台

仲裁委员会席　　　监督委员会席

竞赛

图 1

---

① 全国武术套路竞赛规则，2003 年版。
② 全国传统武术套路竞赛规则，2011 年版。

图 2

说明：

裁判席在主席台对面，裁判员之间要有 50 厘米的间距。

①、②、③、④、⑤为裁判员席

📹 为仲裁摄像机位

★ 为裁判长位

□为副裁判长位

△ 为记录员位

第二部分　装备

太极拳、剑比赛的装备包括器械、服装。

（一）太极剑[①]

必须使用国家体育总局武术运动管理中心指定的器械。

1. 太极剑的结构

剑的结构分为剑身和剑把两段，由以下各部分构成（如图 3 所示）。

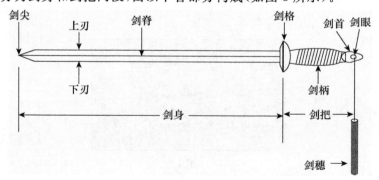

图 3

---

① 武冬.太极剑全书[M].北京：北京体育大学出版社，1999 年 1 月.

2. 太极剑的规格

根据 1991 年《武术竞赛规则》规定,现代武术竞赛用剑剑身变薄,且不开锋刃。

剑的长度:以直臂垂肘,反手持剑的姿势为准,剑尖不得低于本人的耳上端。

剑的重量:包括剑穗,成年男子不得轻于 0.6 千克;成年女子不得轻于 0.5 千克;少年儿童不受限制。

剑的硬度:剑垂直倒置,剑尖触地,剑尖至剑柄加厘米处(测量点),距地面的垂直距离,不得少于 10 厘米(如图 4 所示)。

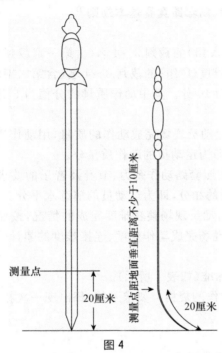

图 4

(二)服装

参加正规太极拳、剑比赛,一般要求穿着太极服。规则在服装的质地、样式方面未作详细规定,由运动员自由选择。一般选择的原则是突出传统文化的特征,样式宽松,有垂感,能够突出太极拳、剑行云流水的演练效果,如图 5 所示。

图 5

基本规则

《全国武术套路竞赛规则》分为自选套路和传统套路两部分。这两部分都包含太极拳、剑项目。因此,目前竞赛的太极拳、剑套路分为自选太极拳、剑和传统太极拳、剑两类。两类套路的评分规则存在一定的差别。下面介绍两类太极拳、剑竞赛的基本规则。

第一部分　自选太极拳、剑套路竞赛基本规则[①]

一、评分方法

(一)由评判动作质量(A组)的裁判3~4名(含第一副裁判长)、评判演练水平(B组)的裁判4名(含裁判长)、评判难度(C组)的裁判3~4名(含第二副裁判长)组成。

(二)各项比赛的满分为10分。其中动作质量的分值为5分,演练水平的分值为3分,难度的分值为2分。

(三)A组裁判员根据运动员现场完成动作的质量,用动作质量的分值减去各种动作规格错误和其他错误的扣分,即为运动员的动作质量分。

(四)B组中由裁判员按照套路动作劲力、节奏及音乐的要求整体评判后确定的等级平均分数减去对套路编排错误的扣分,即为运动员的演练水平分。

(五)C组裁判员根据运动员现场整套难度完成的情况,按照各项目动作难度和连接难度的确认标准,确定运动员现场完成动作难度、连接难度的累计分,即为运动员的难度分。

二、评分标准

(一)动作质量的评分标准(如表1所示)。

运动员现场完成套路动作的规格与要求不符,每出现一次扣0.1分;其他错误每出现一次扣0.1~0.3分。

(二)演练水平的评分标准。

1. 劲力、节奏、音乐的评分标准

分为3档9个分数段,其中:很好为3.00分~2.70分;一般为2.60分~2.30分;较差为2.10分~1.80分。

——凡劲力充足,用力顺达,力点准确,节奏分明,动作与音乐和谐一致者为"很好"。

——凡劲力较充足,用力较顺达,力点较准确,节奏较分明,动作与音乐较和谐一致者为"一般"。

——凡劲力不充足,用力不顺达,力点不准确,节奏不分明,动作与音乐不和谐一致者为"较差"。

2. 编排的评分标准

运动员现场完成套路时,必选的主要动作每缺少一个扣0.2分;套路的结构、布局与要求不符,每出现一次扣0.1分。

(三)难度的评分标准。

1. 动作难度(1.4分)

根据太极拳、剑"动作难度等级内容及分值确定表"(如表2所示),每完成一个A级动作

---

① 全国武术套路竞赛规则,2003年版。

可获得 0.2 分,每完成一个 B 级动作可获得 0.3 分,每完成一个 C 级动作可获得 0.4 分。每个动作难度分只能计算一次;动作难度分的累计中,如超过了 1.4 分,则按 1.4 分计算。

运动员现场所做的动作难度不符合规定要求,则不计算动作难度分。

表 1 自选太极拳、剑动作规格和其他错误内容及扣分标准

内容	扣分点	内容	扣分点
侧朝天蹬直立	支撑腿弯曲或上蹬腿弯曲	上步	前腿支撑时脚外摆超过 45 度、后腿上步时脚拖地
前举腿、后插腿低势平衡	前举腿低于水平或插出腿脚触地		
分脚、蹬脚	支撑腿膝弯曲或上举腿未伸直	挂剑撩剑	直腕
雀地龙	前脚掌内扣触地或两大腿夹角小于 4 度	其他	晃动、脚碾动、移动或跳动
腾空飞脚、旋风脚、外摆	击响腿脚尖未过肩或击拍落空 倒地(扣 0.3)		附加支撑(扣 0.2) 侧倒
腾空正踢腿	悬垂腿弯曲		器械触地、拖把、碰身
仆步	屈蹲腿未全蹲或平仆腿未伸直或全脚掌未内扣着地		器械掉地(扣 0.3)
弓步	前腿膝部未达脚背或超出脚尖		身体任何一部分触及线外地面

注:
① 身体某一部分在空间超越了场地,不应判为出界。
② 未标明扣分点分值的均为扣 0.1 分。
③ "晃动"是指支撑状态时,上体出现的双向位移。
④ "碾动"是指单脚落地时脚掌或脚跟出现的拧动。
⑤ "移动"是指双脚支撑时,任何一脚出现位移。
⑥ "附加支撑"是指由于失去平衡造成手、肘、膝、头部、上臂及非支撑脚触地或借助器械撑地。
⑦ "倒地"是指双手、双膝、肩、躯干、臀部触地。
⑧ 对"水平"的评判,均以被评判部位的垂直轴线为准。
⑨ 对步法、步型和器械方法错误的扣分,均以同类动作组合为单元,每错多次出现只扣一次。

表 2 太极拳、剑动作难度等级及分值确定表

类别	难度等级及加分分值		
	A 级+0.2	B 级+0.3	C 级+0.4
平衡	前举腿低势平衡	后插腿低势平衡	侧朝天蹬直立
腿法	蹬脚或分脚		
跳跃	腾空飞脚	腾空正踢腿 腾空飞脚向内转体 180° 旋风脚 360° 腾空摆莲 360°	旋风脚 540° 腾空摆莲 540°

注:
① 跳跃动作起跳时,只能上一步。
② 腾空正踢腿踢起腿必须是起跳腿;腾空飞脚向内转体 180°、旋风脚 360°、旋风脚 540°落地时必须衔接提膝独立;腾空摆莲 360°、腾空摆莲 540°落地时必须衔接提膝独立、雀地龙,衔接雀地龙应左腿在前。

2. 连接难度(0.6 分)

根据太极拳、剑"连接难度等级内容及加分分值表"(如表 3 所示),每完成一个 A 级连

接可获得0.05分,每完成一个B级连接可获得0.1分,每完成一个C级连接可获得0.15分,每完成一个D级连接可获得0.2分。每个连接难度分只能计算一次,连接难度分的累计中,如超出了0.6分,则按0.6分计算。

表3　连接难度等级内容及加分分值

A级+0.05	B级+0.1	C级+0.15	D级+0.2
腾空飞脚+起跳脚落地	腾空正踢腿+起跳脚落地	腾空摆莲540°+雀地龙	旋风脚540°+提膝独立
	腾空飞脚向内转体180°+提膝独立		
腾空飞脚+提膝独立	旋风脚360°+提膝独立		腾空摆莲540°+提膝独立
腾空摆莲360°+雀地龙	腾空摆莲360°+提膝独立		
腾空飞脚+腾空摆莲360°(无步)	腾空飞脚+腾空摆莲540°(无步)		

运动员现场完成的连接难度不符合规定要求,则不计算连接难度分。

3. 创新难度加分

现场成功完成被确认的创新难度,则由裁判长按加分标准给予加分。

其标准为:完成一个创新的B级动作难度(含连接难度)加0.2分;完成一个创新的C级动作难度(含连接难度)加0.3分;完成一个创新的超C级动作难度加0.4分。

由于失败或与鉴定确认动作难度不符,不予加分。

第二部分　传统太极拳、剑套路基本规则[①]

一、评分方法

(一)裁判员根据运动员现场发挥的技术水平,根据与"等级评分的总体要求"的相符程度,按照等级分的评分标准,并与其他运动员进行比较,确定运动员等级分数;在此基础上,减去其他错误的扣分即为运动员的得分。裁判员评分可到小数点后2位数,尾数为0~9。

(二)应得分数的确定。

3名裁判员评分时,取中间裁判员评出的运动员得分为运动员的应得分;4名裁判员评分时,取中间2名裁判员评出的运动员得分的平均值为运动员的应得分;5名裁判员评分时,取中间3名裁判员评出的运动员得分的平均值为运动员的应得分。应得分可取到小数点后2位数,第3位数不做四舍五入。

(三)裁判长对评分的调整。

当评分中出现明显不合理现象时,在示出运动员最后得分前,裁判长须经总裁判长同意,可调整运动员的应得分。裁判长调整分数范围为0.01分~0.03分。

(四)最后得分的确定。

裁判长从运动员的应得分中减去"裁判长的扣分"和加上"裁判长调整分",即为运动员的最后得分。

二、评分标准

(一)等级分的评分标准。

分为3档9级,其中:8.50分~10.00分为优秀;7.00分~8.49分为良好;5.00分~

---

① 全国传统武术套路竞赛规则,2011年版。

7.00 分为尚可(如表 4 所示)。

表 4　等级评分标准

等别	级别		评分分值
优秀	上	①级	9.50～10.00
优秀	中	②级	9.00～9.49
优秀	下	③级	8.50～8.99
良好	上	④级	8.00～8.49
良好	中	⑤级	7.50～7.99
良好	下	⑥级	7.00～7.49
尚可	上	⑦级	6.50～6.99
尚可	中	⑧级	6.00～6.49
尚可	下	⑨级	5.00～5.99

等级评分的总体要求是：

1. 运动员应表现出所演练的拳种及项目的技术和风格特点，应包含该项目的主要内容，动作规范、方法正确，表现出该项目的主要技法。

2. 劲力顺达，力点准确，通过运动员的肢体以及器械表现出该项目的力法特点；手眼身法步配合协调，器械项目还需身械协调。

3. 节奏恰当，表现出该项目的节奏特点。

4. 结构严密，编排合理，整套动作均应与该项目的技术风格保持一致。

5. 对练还须动作逼真、配合严密、攻防合理。

6. 集体项目还须队形整齐，配合默契并富于变化。

7. 配乐项目的动作与音乐和谐一致，音乐的风格应和该项目的技术风格相一致。

(二) 裁判员执行的其他错误内容及扣分标准(如表 5 所示)。

表 5　其他错误内容及扣分标准

错误种类	错误内容及扣分标准		
	扣 0.1 分	扣 0.2 分	扣 0.3 分
服装、饰物影响动作	◆ 刀剑、剑穗掉地或缠身 ◆ 服装开纽或撕裂 ◆ 服饰、头饰掉地 ◆ 鞋脱落		
器械触地、脱把、碰身、变形、折断、掉地	◆ 器械触地 ◆ 器械脱把 ◆ 器械碰(缠)身 ◆ 器械弯曲变形		◆ 器械折断(含即将折断) ◆ 器械掉地
出界	◆ 身体任一部位触及线外地面		
失去平衡	◆ 上体晃动、脚移动或跳动	◆ 手、肘、膝、足、器械的附加支撑	◆ 倒地(双手或肩、头、躯干、臀部触地)
遗忘	◆ 遗忘一次		
对练项目特殊错误	◆ 击打落空	◆ 误中对方	◆ 误伤对方

注：运动员在一次失误中若出现多种表中列举的错误，累计扣分。

（三）裁判长执行的其他错误内容及扣分标准。

1. 完成套路时间不足或超出规定。凡不足规定时间达 2 秒以内扣 0.1 分，达 4 秒以内扣 0.2 分，达 4 秒以上，最多扣 0.3 分；凡超出规定时间达 5 秒以内扣 0.1 分，达 10 秒以内扣 0.2 分，达 10 秒以上，最多扣 0.3 分。

2. 集体项目的人数，少于竞赛规程规定的人数，每少 1 人，扣 0.5 分。

3. 配乐不符合竞赛规程规定者，扣 0.5 分。

自选太极拳与传统太极拳在规则上的明显不同之处就在于：自选太极拳有难度动作的评分。而且有研究者表明，近年来难度动作完成的质量直接决定着比赛的名次。这也导致了运动员花费大部分时间练习难度动作，从而造成动作质量和演练水平的下降，这也使得有人批评自选项目"异化"为舞蹈、体操。但是，增加难度动作的优点是使得比赛更加客观，更容易量化，提高了比赛的公正性。传统太极拳、剑的比赛则更加注重突出传统武术的传统性、技击性和观赏性，但规则的客观性程度明显不如自选太极拳、剑。对于演练类的武术套路竞赛，保持项目的特点与提高竞赛的客观性似乎成为不可调和的矛盾，至少目前看来，还没有很好的解决办法。

参考文献

[1] 李德印.太极拳入门与提高[M].北京：人民体育出版社,1999.

[2] 杨澄甫.太极拳体用全书[M].北京：人民体育出版社,1957.

[3] 周稔丰.太极拳常识[M].北京：人民体育出版社,1978.

[4] 中华人民共和国体育运动委员会运动词.太极拳运动[M].北京：人民体育出版社,1978.

[5] 郑勤.太极文化与功法[M].武汉：湖北人民出版社,2004.

[6] 北京大学体育教研部.太极拳·剑入门捷径[M].北京：北京体育大学出版社,1996.

[7] 沈寿.太极拳法研究[M].福州：福建人民出版社,1984.

[8] 李德印.太极拳入门与提高[M].北京：人民体育出版社,1999.

[9] 李成银.试论中国武术文化的结构[J].体育科学,1992,(4)：19-21.

[10] 田桂菊.析太极拳的文化价值观[J].成都体育学院学报,2007,33(5)：44.

[11] 马斌.弘扬太极文化营造和谐环境[J].焦作大学学报,2006,(4)：28.

[12] 高丽.试论中国古代儒道家哲学思想对太极拳的影响[J].搏击：武术科学,2008,5(3)：26-27.

[13] 朱继华,程梅.太极拳的文化内涵在体育素质教育中的作用[J].南京体育学院学报,2004,18(6)：64-65.

[14] 杜晓红,李强.对周易与太极拳内在联系的探讨[J].体育与科学,2008,29(2)：58-5.

[15] 武冬.太极拳教学与训练英汉双语教程[M].北京：北京体育大学出版社,2009.

[16] 刘玉萍.24式太极拳连续练习一套三套对老年人心血管机能的影响[J].北京体育大学学报,1996(3)：41-46.

[17] 李杰,郝光安.24式太极拳[EB/OL].[2016-1-10].http：//pe.pku.edu.cn/pkuped/jpkc/resources/tjqvcd/main/main.html.

[18] 太极网：http//www.taiji.net.cn.

[19] 钱塘太极网：http//qttjw.com.